eBay 2024

A Beginner's Guide to E-commerce Success

Acknowledgments

This book is dedicated to my parents, Bernard and Darline Vulich, who taught me the joy of reading early in my life. They ensured I had frequent access to a bookstore, whether the local Guzzardo's Book Nook in Clinton or Readmore Book World in Rock Island. If I never said it, thanks!

The cover was designed by Tori Vulich. Thanks again for creating another great design.

(This cover has been designed using assets from FreePix.com and RawPixel.com.)

Table of Contents

Introduction

I n today's fast-paced and interconnected world, eBay is like a treasure chest brimming with opportunities just waiting to be cracked open. And guess what? **eBay 2024** isn't just a guide; it's an adventure. Together, we will embark on a journey to unearth the secrets and strategies that can transform ordinary folks into eBay superstars. Imagine your journey as a thrilling treasure hunt through the digital marketplace.

Whether you're a seasoned eBay pro looking to boost your sales or new to the game, this book will guide you every step of the way. It's packed with valuable tips, real-life success stories, and hands-on advice to ensure you're fully equipped for success in the eBay universe.

eBay 2024 isn't holding back - it covers everything from selecting the right products, crafting listings that grab attention, and delivering exceptional customer service to demystifying eBay's algorithms and staying at the forefront of ever-evolving e-commerce trends. We're leaving no stone unturned to ensure you're ready to take on the eBay scene with confidence.

Now is the time to seize the opportunities that eBay presents, tap into its vast potential, and set sail on a path toward financial independence and entrepreneurial glory in the digital age. It's your moment to become an eBay maestro and unlock countless opportunities in this dynamic online marketplace.

As we delve deeper into **eBay 2024**, you'll become intimately acquainted with the eBay world. We'll guide you through setting up your own eBay store, making your listings stand out from the crowd and mastering pricing strategies that keep customers coming back for more.

But this isn't just a how-to book; it's your personal guide to conquering the e-commerce universe. You'll learn how to manage your inventory like a pro, handle customer inquiries with the finesse of a champion, and cultivate a customer-friendly approach that keeps the orders flowing in.

In today's digital age, data is as good as gold. We'll explore the power of analytics and teach you how to harness data to make eBay work for you. We'll crack the code of eBay's algorithms and unveil the secrets of search engine optimization to ensure your listings are seen by the right audience.

But it's not all business talk; we'll dive into the mindset and skills needed to not just survive but thrive. You'll learn how to adapt to market trends, embrace change, and stay one step ahead of your competitors. And you'll find inspiration in the stories of eBay pros who've faced challenges, grown their businesses, and made their dreams come true.

eBay 2024 is your personal GPS to selling successfully on eBay, offering not only practical tips but also the inspiration and motivation you need to thrive in this vibrant online world. It's time to transform your eBay aspirations into reality, embark on an exciting adventure, and unlock the immense potential of eBay selling. **eBay 2024** is your ultimate treasure map to navigate these online waters and discover your pot of gold.

Getting Started

Selling stuff on eBay is no walk in the park. It's not everyone's cup of tea, and there's no guarantee that you'll be rolling in the dough. I'm not here to sugarcoat it because not many folks are upfront about the hurdles.

The truth is that it can be a bit of a rollercoaster ride. If you're already hustling on eBay, you've probably had your share of ups and downs. And if you're a newbie in the eBay game, keep in mind that it's not all smooth sailing from the get-go.

Most books on online selling make it sound like once you list your items, you can kick back in your PJs, watch your favorite shows, and watch the cash flow 24/7. Ah, if only it were that simple! But that's not the case.

Here's the scoop: the more time you spend on eBay, the smoother things tend to get. You'll start making more sales, and folks will keep coming back for more if you offer them good deals and top-notch customer service. But here's the kicker – it's still a bit of a wild ride, whether you're a seasoned pro or a fresh face in the eBay arena.

Sales go up and down with the seasons, my friend. The summer months can be slower than a sloth, but come the Christmas season, the eBay sales machine revs up. Many eBay sellers make a good chunk of their moolah during the holiday frenzy. Where you land on this rollercoaster depends on what kind of goods you're selling.

The dream is to find a mix of products that keeps sales ticking along so you don't get slammed with wild fluctuations. But hey, it doesn't just happen by magic; you've got to plan it out and mix it into your selling strategy.

And, oh, let me tell you about those times when you've been selling the same stuff for years, and suddenly, it's like someone hit the pause button. Sales drop, and it feels like you're in a ghost town. What's the deal, you ask? Did a new kid on the block start slashing prices, making your stuff seem too pricey? Did some fancy new gizmo hit the scene, making your products look like relics? Or did too many folks hop on the bandwagon and flood the market?

Whatever the case, you've got to act fast. Otherwise, you're stuck beating a dead horse. Hopefully, you've got a Plan B up your sleeve.

And that, my friend, is where this book comes in. I'm going to spill the beans on how to navigate eBay today and tomorrow. To truly make it, you've got to be nimble, adaptable, and ready to face whatever curveballs eBay throws your way.

Here's the deal: I'm not going to drop any secret gems on you, and this ain't rocket science. It's all about rolling up your sleeves, putting in the hard work, and relying on a good dose of common sense.

So, buckle up because if you can ace five key areas, you're well on your way to becoming an eBay superstar, ready for whatever today, tomorrow, and the future may bring.

1. Plan for success
2. Establish a Niche
3. Ship like a pro
4. Sell international
5. Know your numbers

Why listen to me?

H ey there, Nick Vulich here.

Think of me as kind of like the "eBay guru," but without the long white beard and the mystical cave.

I'm the guy you turn to when you're looking to make a few extra bucks or maybe even start a small online business without all the confusing jargon. I mean, who wants to decipher a textbook when you can read one of my down-to-earth guides on how to sell stuff on eBay and other online platforms?

Some readers have likened my books to treasure maps, but instead of "X marks the spot," it's more like "Listings and Keywords" mark the spot. My writing style makes it easy to understand the ins and outs of e-commerce.

So, next time you stumble upon a stack of old records or a collection of vintage postcards, remember my books are your go-to roadmap to turning those finds into dollars – and they do it all with a casual, light-hearted touch that makes learning about e-commerce a breeze. It's like getting advice from your friendly neighborhood e-commerce expert!

But seriously, I've written more than a dozen books about how to sell on eBay, Amazon, Etsy, Fiverr, and other online platforms.

My first book, *Freaking Idiots Guide to Selling on eBay*, is still a bestseller on Amazon. I followed that one up with *eBay Unleashed* and *Sell It Online*. And then, in 2014, I began my series of yearly eBay guides. *eBay 2015* was the most popular, and for that reason I've chosen to update it for 2024.

eBay 2024 is a mix of old and new. It still contains much of the information people enjoyed in 2015, but it's been updated to provide the info you need to sell on eBay today. Besides the usual details about how to sell on eBay, this book delves into shipping and accounting—two areas sellers need to nail to succeed in e-commerce. It also includes bonus chapters about how to get started selling on Amazon and Fiverr.

Let's get started...

$5,000 a Month Selling on eBay

S ounds impossible, doesn't it?

I'm here to tell you I have done it—and so have thousands of other sellers.

You can, too!

It's just a matter of getting started.

New sellers ask me every day, "What's the secret to selling on eBay?" or "What's the best way to get started selling on Amazon?"

I tell them what I'm going to tell you.

"Get started. "

List your first item today. Don't worry about what you don't know or what you think you need to know.

"Just do it!"

It really is that simple. I can tell you everything I know about how to sell on eBay. I can tell you what products to sell. I can tell you how much to charge and what type of listing template to use. I can tell you the best time to start and end your listings, how to ship your items, and on—and on.

But there's one thing I can't do.

I can't make you get started.

Think about that for a moment. Every day, hundreds of people buy guides just like this one. They read them from cover to cover. Many of them underline important passages and scribble notes in the margins or on a notepad.

They plan what they're going to do, sell, and how much money they are going to make.

And, then...they begin to doubt themselves. They ask themselves questions—like, what if it doesn't work? What if I list my items wrong? What if my items don't sell? What will I tell my friends if I fail?

Does any of this sound familiar?

What I'm trying to help you understand here is simple. We are all plagued by self-doubt. Everybody questions things when they are first getting started with something new. What you need to do if you want to become successful is to overcome these doubts.

It's like learning to walk. You put one foot in front of the other and keep moving. If you fall down—you dust yourself off and keep moving.

Selling online is like learning to walk.

You try one product or one listing. If your item doesn't sell, you find another one and try again. If your item sells, you tweak your description or product so that you can sell even more.

If you don't learn anything else from reading this book, keep this one bit of information in the back of your mind.

Success is all about getting started.

Why you should sell on eBay & Amazon

Bay and Amazon are the e-commerce giants of the world. These two bad boys pull in over 150 billion bucks in sales every year and boast an impressive 400 million registered users. What's even sweeter is that they let you tap into that massive user base to peddle your goods and services.

So, if you're just a regular Joe or Jane looking to dive into the online biz world, eBay and Amazon are the easiest ways to dip your toes in. You don't need to be an SEO whiz, a blogger or waste your hard-earned cash on those pricey PPC ads on Google or Facebook. Nope, all you gotta do is toss your item up on eBay or Amazon, and boom, you're in business!

If you're new to online selling, eBay and Amazon are the ultimate training wheels. Amazon, in particular, is like catching a ride on someone else's business. Find a listing that's similar to your product, hit that "Sell on Amazon" button next to the "Have one to sell?" line, and follow the prompts to add your item's condition and price. Voila, you're an Amazon seller!

And don't sweat it if you stumble upon something totally unique that no one's listed before. Amazon has a tool for that, and we'll dive into it later in this guide.

Now, keep in mind Amazon does have a few rules about what you can sell, especially during the holiday season. They don't want the little guys competing with their big-shot merchants. So, you might run into a situation where your listing is kind of in the shadows. It's still there, but only you and Amazon can see it. Sneaky, right?

eBay offers a similar deal. If you're looking to sell, just click on the "Have one to sell?" text, and you're on your way to creating a snazzy listing page. It's not as straightforward as Amazon's method, but with a little tweaking, you can make a pretty slick listing. eBay requires at least one picture of your product and lets you jazz up the description to better match what you're selling, like talking about the color of any accessories or any minor wear and tear.

Like Amazon, eBay allows you to create new listings from scratch if you're dealing with a truly unique item. We'll dig deeper into that in another chapter. For now, remember that eBay and Amazon are pretty flexible in how you can list and sell your stuff. The method you choose should depend on what you're selling, where you're selling it, and your sales goals. So, get out there and start making some online sales magic!

Which site should you sell on?

Sometimes, deciding whether to go with eBay or Amazon to sell your products can be a bit of a puzzle. But don't worry. There are some handy guidelines to help you make the right choice.

eBay is your go-to when you're dealing with unique, pricier items or when you're not quite sure about the item's value. If you've got multiple copies of something, eBay's auction feature is your playground. It lets you test the waters and even snag a higher price for those uncertain or unpriced items. Worried you won't get the right price? No sweat set a reserve price, and if it doesn't hit that mark, the item won't sell.

On the flip side, Amazon is perfect for everyday items like books, clothes, shoes, cell phones, and electronics. If your item is a consistent seller with a clear price range, Amazon is the spot. Plus, they don't hit you with listing fees – they only get a slice when your item sells.

Now, let's talk about fees. eBay and Amazon both have their own fee structures. eBay's final value fees have rolled in payment processing fees since they've embraced Managed Payments. Meanwhile, Amazon skips listing fees entirely and earns a cut when your item sells. If you're an eBay store owner, you get some free listings each month and a discount for extras.

Here's where Amazon shines – they make it super easy to figure out how fast your items should move. They rank every product based on its sales performance. Take books, for example. They've got millions listed, and each has a product ranking. Lower rankings mean better sales — books under 100 are hotcakes, under 10,000 are steady, and under 50,000 still move a few copies every week. Once you've cracked the Amazon ranking code, it's a breeze to pick the winners.

eBay takes a tad more detective work to ferret out the winners. Use their advanced search function to see how many of a particular item sold recently and what they went for. Keep using this info, and you'll get better at sourcing fast-selling stuff for your listings. So, there you have it: eBay for the unique and experimental, and Amazon for the tried and true!

Getting Started on eBay

Almost every writer starts their talk about selling on eBay by going on about what to sell or how to sell, but they're overlooking the most crucial part of being successful on eBay: building a solid reputation. If your feedback isn't top-notch, you're going to have a hard time boosting your sales.

If you're new to this whole eBay buying and selling thing, here's the deal: both buyers and sellers rate each other using a five-star system. Now, this system kinda tilts in favor of the buyers because if they're not happy, they can drop some negative feedback for the seller. Sellers, on the other hand, can't do the same to buyers anymore.

When potential buyers are eyeballing your stuff, they're gonna check out your feedback rating to decide if it's safe to buy from you. If two sellers are offering the same thing for about the same price, buyers will go with the one who's got the better feedback. It just makes sense to spend your cash with someone who's got a good rep.

So, your main goal here is to make sure your customers are over the moon with their purchases and leave you some awesome feedback. Sounds simple, right? Well, let's dive into a couple of examples that can make buyers want to leave that not-so-great feedback.

When folks buy stuff on eBay, the site gives them an estimated delivery time. The top-rated sellers are supposed to ship their items within 24 hours to make sure things arrive on time. But sometimes, the postal service does its own thing, and packages show up late, even though it's not the seller's fault. That's when unhappy buyers might drop some negative feedback, even though it's not fair.

Now, here's the deal. Sometimes, buyers get cold feet before the seller even ships the item. Back in the day, sellers could just ask to cancel the sale, and if the buyer agreed, everything was fine. But eBay's defect system makes it tricky today. If a buyer changes their mind, it puts the seller in a tight spot. They have to choose between giving good customer service and canceling the sale or saying, "Sorry, you'll have to talk to eBay about that." The thing is, if the buyer requests the cancellation, the seller doesn't get a black mark. But here's the kicker — if the seller waits for eBay to sort it out, they might miss their shipping deadline. That's a seller defect, and too many of those can get you kicked off eBay.

Oh, and here's another one. Sometimes, customers buy something and ask the seller to hold off on shipping it until they come back from vacation or closer to someone's birthday. Being a good seller means accommodating that request, but eBay sees it as a seller defect.

These are just some of the sticky situations you'll face when trying to balance top-notch customer service with keeping your defect rate low on eBay. I can't give you a one-size-fits-all solution for these issues. You'll have to figure it out case by case.

So, that's the lowdown on customer service. When you're selling on eBay, it's all about making product listings that really get people excited about what you're offering.

When you create your listings, you need to...

Create a title loaded with keywords.

When it comes to eBay listings, your title is the ticket to getting noticed.

With just 80 characters to describe your product, every word counts. But here's the secret sauce many sellers overlook: your title is a treasure trove of search terms.

It's what helps potential buyers discover your item among the sea of eBay listings. So, don't squander those precious characters – make each keyword in your title pack a punch.

How, you ask?

Simple. Put yourself in the buyer's shoes. What words would you use to search for that item? What really matters to you? Think manufacturer, model number, color, condition (new, used, refurbished), free shipping, and easy returns.

Take large, well-lit photos.

eBay is fast becoming a visual experience. The internet is a visual wonderland, with cat videos, funny photos, and captivating illustrations taking center stage. What does this mean for you, the online seller?

It means you've got to step up your photo game.

Your listings need large, crystal-clear photos that showcase your product from every angle. If there's any damage, zoom in and provide close-ups.

Your pictures should be so lifelike that customers feel they could reach out and touch your merchandise. Just like that Fiverr cover designer who proudly claims that the chocolate on her covers looks good enough to eat, your photos should be so enticing that they practically jump off the screen and into your customers' hands.

Trust me, if you do this, you'll be raking in more cash than ever before.

Write a benefit-driven description.

Most sellers recite all the droll facts that describe what they are selling. "I have a yellow taxi cab from 1964. It has an AM radio, bald tires, a spare tire, and oh yeah—it only runs when you can get a few friends together to give it a push." Slightly humorous but dull. It doesn't contain anything that compels you to buy the yellow taxi.

You need to create listings that mimic the way people read on the internet. Most people read the headlines and then skim through the copy, looking for details that interest them. If you list your key points using bullet points, your customer's eyes are going to move directly from the headlines to the bullet points.

Another mistake sellers make is rambling off a slew of features. Customers could care less about features. They want to know what's in it for them.

Tell them the benefits.

- Your new TV comes equipped with a full-featured remote, so you never need to get out of your chair to change the channel or adjust the volume.
- Your new theater chairs are awesome. They have a built-in refrigerator and urination control system, so you never miss a moment of programming to grab another beer or go number one.

Research your item and price it to sell.

While some inexperienced sellers rush into posting their listings without a second thought, savvy online sellers know that thorough research is the key to unlocking more profits.

Here's the lowdown: before you hit that "list" button, take some time to dive into the details of your item.

Get to know it inside and out. Understand how likely it is to sell, the reasonable price range you can expect to get for it, and the golden keywords that will make your listing pop.

Remember, eBay's top-tier sellers have cracked the code – the more effort and research you invest in your item, the more money you'll make.

Manage buyer expectations.

Managing buyer expectations is crucial. Think of your listing as a journey for potential buyers. You want to take them on an exciting adventure, making them picture themselves using your item. However, before sealing the deal, you need to hit the brakes for a moment. Let them in on any hiccups or blemishes your item might have.

Be upfront about the good, the bad, and the ugly. Honesty is the name of the game. Whether it's a scratch on a smartphone or compatibility issues with a device, lay it all out there. You might be thinking, "Won't this scare off potential buyers?" The surprising truth is that it often has the opposite effect.

When you take the time to explain any defects or potential issues, buyers are more likely to trust you. They appreciate your transparency and are more confident in their decision to buy.

Make These Changes First

B ased on my experience selling on eBay, there are a few moves sellers can make to up their game.

If you're a seller on the verge of a breakthrough, these changes might just be the nudge you need to hit the big time. And if you're new to the selling game, there's no better time to kick things off on the right foot. You don't have any pesky habits to unlearn, so dive in and get started.

Keep in mind—this is stuff that has worked for me with the items I sell. Not everything will work for you. Keep doing what works for you—adjust or discard the rest.

Remove all HTML code from your listings.

eBay's Cassini Search doesn't really get along with HTML code, especially when it's lurking in your listing header. I mean, don't get me wrong, I'm a fan of fancy listing templates with snazzy designs and picture-perfect formatting, but you know what I like even more? That sweet sound of my eBay app's cash register ringing.

So, here's a little trick: when your sales are in a slump, and nothing seems to be working, try stripping out the fancy headers and all that stylish formatting from a few listings. See what happens. If your plain, unadorned listings start bringing in more sales, then that's the way to roll. It's all about figuring out what works best for you.

Check your listing on your smartphone.

Mobile is where it's at. Everyone is glued to their phones, tablets, and Kindles, constantly checking for emails, tweets, and Facebook updates. Last Christmas, more than sixty percent of the holiday shopping action happened on mobile devices. This year, it's expected to be even higher, around seventy percent.

If you don't make your listings mobile-friendly, you will miss out on more than half of the potential customers. So, once you're done listing items, pull out your smartphone or iPad and give your listings a once-over. Check that they show up in search and are optimized for mobile viewing.

If you insert your photos using fancy HTML or listing apps like Auctiva or Ink Frog, your pics might end up tiny and hard to see. But if you use eBay's listing page, your images will fill the whole screen, and potential buyers can easily swipe through them.

Ask yourself, which format would you be more likely to buy from? Then, make the necessary changes to up your eBay game.

Get straight to the point. Less is better.

People are always in a rush these days, and the key to selling more stuff is making it super easy for them to buy from you.

Let's face it: folks can be a bit lazy. They skim through auction descriptions just like they skim through blog posts and other internet content. They're looking for those attention-grabbing words, they check out bullet points for a quick overview, and they take a peek at picture captions.

But here's the kicker: if they stumble upon a giant wall of text, they'll hit that back-arrow button and move on to the next listing. That's where white space, bullet points, and bold headings become your trusty sidekicks in the quest for more sales.

Include more and better pictures.

When it comes to pictures, don't hold back. More than half of buyers make their decision solely based on the images in your listing. They might not have the time or the desire to read your item description, and some international buyers might not even understand it.

They rely on your pictures to make up their minds. So, give them lots of close-ups and nudge them to use the pics to decide if the item fits their needs.

Focus on the 80 /20 rule.

Concentrate your efforts on selling the top 20% of items that bring in the most profit. Ditch the slow sellers. If you're like most sellers, just a handful of your items make up the bulk of your sales.

If you've got an eBay store, you probably have loads of items gathering dust. Maybe a dozen or so sell each month, but the rest just hang around, eating up your free listings and costing you extra fees. They might even tempt you into working extra hours in hopes of making that one elusive sale.

Enough with the long shots. Aim for the sure things.

Put your focus on the top 20% of items that are your best sellers. Don't waste your precious time and money on listings that hardly ever move.

It's all about working smarter, not harder.

Don't try to reinvent the wheel.

Discovering a new, hot-selling product that's in a league of its own is fantastic. However, those gems are rare. If you pour all your energy into hunting for the next big thing, you might miss out on consistent earners.

Sure, we all daydream about being the pioneer of the Hula Hoop or the Pet Rock, but those opportunities are one in a million. Focusing solely on long shots can make you overlook the steady wins you could have along the way.

Catching a wave with a new trend can indeed make you rich and famous, but selling dependable items like denim jackets or vintage toys keeps the cash flowing day in and day out. These are the ones that put food on the table and gas in your tank.

Chasing trends can burn through your listing fees, your time that could be spent posting profitable items, and the free time you'd rather spend with your family and friends.

Don't beat a dead horse. Items run out of gas.

Products can lose their appeal and stop selling for various reasons. Know when it's time to call it quits and venture into a new niche.

Sometimes, good things come to an end.

I've been peddling vintage magazine articles, prints, and advertisements for the past fifteen years, and they've been sputtering along since the 2008 recession. eBay's shift to fixed-price listings hasn't helped. Sales are down, prices are down, and profits are down.

I'm beating a dead horse.

It's a tough decision. We've been through a lot in fifteen years. There's still some money coming in, sometimes thousands of dollars a month, but it's not what it used to be.

My challenge for 2024 is to reinvent my business and find a new niche. What about you? If you're in a similar boat, do you have a plan to either move on or breathe new life into what you're doing?

Spend more time on customer follow-up.

Invest more time in customer follow-up. Engage in some casual chit-chat. Shoot the breeze. It's a simple way to build a rapport with your customers and boost your sales.

Getting to know your customers doesn't have to be time-consuming. Just make it a routine part of your business day.

When someone asks about an item you're selling, take a moment to answer their question. Express your gratitude for their inquiry. Share some enthusiasm about your item and your product lineup. Ask them how they plan to use the product and what other items they'd like to see you offer.

If it's around a holiday, extend warm wishes like "Merry Christmas!" or "Happy Easter!" If you prefer to keep it neutral, offer a "happy holiday season" greeting.

Building a connection with your customers takes just a few minutes, but it leaves them with a positive feeling about doing business with you.

Try new things.

Embrace novelty. Complacency has been the downfall of many businesses.

Challenge yourself to introduce at least one new product each week. Even if only a handful succeed by the year's end, you'll have a more robust product lineup.

Products and entire product lines can go stale. They become outdated, just like people who cling to the past. Think about those folks from high school or college who are still reminiscing about their glory days. It's nice to share a few memories, but then you start to realize that they're stuck.

Products are similar; they can get stuck in a certain era. Unless you're specializing in nostalgia, it's essential to cut those strings and explore new opportunities. This will not only strengthen your product lineup but also challenge you to become a better seller.

Take Buyer Protection Cases seriously.

When a buyer protection case is opened against you, it's essential to set aside any personal feelings and suspicions that the customer might be trying to take advantage of you. Instead, act promptly by offering a full refund, especially for lower-value items. Not only will this decision make you feel better, but it will also enhance your reputation with your customers and eBay.

Think of it this way: in the grand scheme of things, what's twenty, fifty, or even a hundred dollars compared to your overall eBay sales?

While you may be in the right, and the customer could be pushing boundaries, it's not worth risking your search ranking or jeopardizing your selling privileges. Take a step back, consider the bigger picture, and do what's best for your business.

Don't allow personal feelings to drag you down.

Give yourself some well-deserved time off.

Selling on eBay is demanding, with customers reaching out around the clock. It can become a relentless cycle of listing new items and shipping old ones within tight deadlines.

Taking breaks to unwind is crucial. eBay can be a challenging gig, but remember, there's always one more item to list, one more package to ship, and one more email to respond to. If you don't set aside some time for yourself, it can take a toll and age you prematurely.

Prioritize self-care before you become the hermit in your eBay dungeon.

Consider selling for charity.

eBay Giving Works makes it easy to sell for a charitable cause.

Choose a national or local charity that resonates with you. Incorporate two or three charity auctions into your monthly listings. This not only improves your own outlook on eBay but also makes your customers feel good about buying from you. It can also boost your earnings.

While not every charity listing will result in a sale or a higher selling price, they tend to attract a significant number of page views.

For example, my regular listings receive twenty to twenty-five page views, but when I add a charity component, they garner several hundred page views, especially when I collaborate with a large national charity.

Charitable listings can increase your sales and profits.

Leverage the "Send Customer Offers" feature. It's a relatively new addition, and I've been using it regularly for almost a year with great results. Here's the scoop: every time someone watches an item, eBay allows you to send them a special offer.

Typically, I mark my items down by about ten to fifteen percent. I send around one hundred offers a week, and anywhere from eight to fifteen buyers take the bait and hit that buy button with an average sale of $20, including shipping, which adds up to an extra $150 to $300 per week.

Not bad for just a few minutes of work.

To get started, hover your cursor over "My eBay" on your PC and click on "Selling." Over to the left, you'll see various options under "Tasks," including "Offers." Click on "Offers" and follow the prompts.

You'll also have the option to allow counteroffers. It can lead to more sales but be prepared for some lowball offers that might make you want to pull your hair out.

If you prefer using the eBay app, go to "My eBay," select "Selling," and click on an item if available offers are shown. Give it a shot – I believe you'll be pleased with the results.

End your items regularly. eBay's search algorithm favors newly listed items.

If you have an eBay store with hundreds or thousands of fixed-price listings, it's a good idea to end them often. It might be a bit of a hassle, but it pays off in the long run.

Having a steady supply of newly listed items ensures that your products remain fresh in the search results. Each time you relist an item, it gets a boost in search rankings, resulting in more sales.

I relist my inventory five or six times a month, and sometimes I make a quick $400 or $500 in the following days, while other times it's just $100. It doesn't matter because the extra money is always welcome, and my items are constantly getting refreshed, ensuring that more buyers will see them.

Plan for Success

Many newcomers to eBay dive headfirst into the platform without a solid plan in place. It's like trying to swim before you learn how to float. Rushing in without understanding the eBay market is a recipe for frustration and disappointment.

Some rookies jump right in and start selling without taking the time to grasp the lay of the land. Others are just plain sloppy – they upload poorly lit photos and create vague descriptions that leave buyers scratching their heads. To make matters worse, in their eagerness to post listings, many sellers end up either overpricing or underpricing their items.

The consequences of these hasty actions can be frustrating. If they overprice, their items gather dust on the virtual shelves, and they're quick to label eBay as a scam that duped them out of their money. On the flip side, if they underprice and their items sell like hotcakes, they're left grumbling about how they can't seem to make any money.

So, if you're thinking about taking the eBay plunge, remember – a little preparation goes a long way. Don't be a hasty eBay seller. Take the time to understand the platform, present your items in the best light, and price them right. Your eBay journey is bound to be a smoother and more profitable one.

....

Selling on eBay is a blend of science and art. I can teach you the scientific side of it. But, to truly succeed, you've got to understand the art of eBay selling, which I like to call "gut instincts."

When you're out hunting for inventory, you should be able to walk into a room and instantly spot the moneymakers. It's like having a sixth sense for what's valuable.

Let me give you an example from my own experience.

I specialize in selling books, magazines, and paper memorabilia. So, when I step into an estate sale, I'm laser-focused on finding vintage magazines. I have a mental list of about twenty-five titles I always grab, but what really gets me excited is discovering something entirely new, something I've never come across before. The more pictures those magazines have, the more I want them.

But here's the secret sauce: I also keep my eyes peeled for items that aren't typically in my wheelhouse but could complement my product line. You see if something unique and intriguing catches my eye, chances are it'll do the same for my niche buyers.

Remember what Mike on "American Pickers" said: "In my business, if you come across something you've never seen before, the best time to buy it is now."

Why is this gut instinct so crucial? Well, if you lack that knack for spotting treasure, it's like walking into a room wearing blinders. There could be fifty items that could double or triple your money, but you'd miss every single one of them because you're too fixated on your comfort zone.

That might be great for the person right behind you, who snatches up all the opportunities you walked past, paying his bills and more. But for you, it sucks. You'd likely end up thinking eBay is a scam and that no one can really make money on the platform. And trust me, you'll find plenty of folks complaining and griping about eBay's supposed evils on forums and blogs. But here's the kicker – it's not eBay. It's you. It's your mindset and attitude.

The sooner you grasp that your eBay success hinges on your approach, the closer you'll get to achieving your goals.

Let me share a personal story to drive this point home. I used to be a traveling salesman, covering a four-state region for years. During my travels, I'd sneak in some eBay sales between meetings and calls. I was making a decent $1500 to $2000 profit each month, but it wasn't life-changing money.

Then, one day, I got a call from the VP of sales telling me they were eliminating my position. They offered me a severance package, promised not to contest my unemployment claim, and even gave me a good reference. All they wanted in return was for me to sign a paper saying I wouldn't sue them.

What could I do? I took the deal. It was a turning point. I decided to take eBay more seriously and transform it into a full-time gig.

So, if you've been daydreaming, now's the time to tune back in. I made a serious commitment to selling on eBay. I was already making decent money, but if I was going to make a living from it, I needed to double or even triple my earnings before my unemployment and severance pay ran out. I had about six months to turn "so-so" into "oh-boy!"

To achieve that, I had to plan seriously.

Make a Plan

Anybody can make a few sales on eBay. The key to success is to keep those sales growing while at the same time discovering new products to sell and new avenues to make your offerings available through.

Doing this isn't as easy as it sounds.

To be successful selling on eBay, or anywhere else for that matter, you need to have a plan, and you need to work your plan.

For me, one of the hardest parts of making a plan was already filled in. I knew what I wanted to sell—historical memorabilia and collectibles.

So, I knew the what.

I also knew where. I wanted to sell my items on eBay.

That left the who, the why, and the how. If I planned on being successful, I needed to connect all of the dots.

That meant answering the who's.

1. Who are my customers?
2. Who is my competition?

I needed to answer the whys.

1. Why do customers buy the stuff I sell?
2. Why should these customers buy from me instead of from another eBay store?

I also had to understand the hows.

1. How do I list my items for maximum impact?

2. How am I going to ship my items—both economically and safely?
3. How am I going to find a steady supply of products to sell so I can keep my business growing?

To put together an effective business plan, you need to answer all of the above questions.

I was lucky. I already knew what I wanted to sell. A lot of newbies stumble when asked that question. For many new sellers, uncertainty about what to sell is the major stumbling block that keeps them from becoming successful.

I'm going to cover that topic in much more detail in the section about how to discover your niche. For now, we're going to concentrate on answering the other questions posed above.

Who are my customers, and why should they buy from me

If you're already selling on eBay, it's going to be much easier to answer these questions. The best way to do this is to ask your customers directly. Every time you send out a customer service email, include a brief survey.

It can be as simple as,

Thanks again for making your purchase from history-bytes. We realize you have lots of options to choose from when purchasing historical collectibles on eBay, so the fact you chose to do business with us is a great honor.

Please take a few moments to check your items over carefully when they arrive and make sure they meet your expectations. Should you have any questions or concerns, please feel free to contact me personally. I will be happy to do whatever I can to make it right for you.
Could I also ask a small favor?
Here at history-bytes, we are always trying to make your shopping experience more enjoyable. Would you have a few moments to tell us about your experiences with history-bytes and why you chose the particular items you did?
It will help us accomplish two important tasks:

1. *It will help us ensure a pleasant shopping experience for our customers.*
2. *It will help us to select more products that our customers want and need.*

To make it as easy as possible, just click reply to this email and tell us what you like or don't like about shopping with history-bytes. Next, tell us a little bit about why you purchased your item and how you intend to use it. Finally, tell us what other items you would like to see us carry.
Thanks again for making your purchase from history-bytes. If you took the time to complete our survey—you're amazing. Rest assured, we will use that info to make your shopping experience with history-bytes even better.
Have a great day!

That's all there is to it. Take our survey. Make it your own. Feel free to change it up a bit and personalize it for your business. Ask about specific products, different parts of the shopping experience, or what customers liked or didn't like about your eBay store or listings.

You will be surprised by what you learn. It just may help you rocket your sales to a new level.

....

If you are new to eBay and don't have any customers to survey, you need to work things a little differently. Most of your research should focus on analyzing sales trends and using your gut instincts to determine how that data affects you.

The first thing you need to do is conduct an advanced search for items similar to what you plan to sell.

If you have never run an advanced search before—don't panic. It's super easy to do. Look for the search box at the top of the eBay page. Just to the right of it, you will see the word "advanced." Click on it.

This takes you to the advanced search page. I know it seems overwhelming at first, but you will figure it out quickly.

The most important thing you need to understand is the only information that counts is what you find in sold listings. Anybody can list anything they want on eBay and ask for a crazy amount of money. The way we separate the wheat from the chaff and get to the good stuff is by analyzing completed sales where people spent money to buy something.

This tells us the seller did something right with their listing.

If you're with me so far.

Pick an item you are interested in selling and run an advanced search. Count how many items sold in the last thirty days (hint: they are listed in green). Now count how many didn't sell (hint: they are listed in red). Divide the number that sold by the total number of items that were listed. Doing this tells you the percentage of items that closed successfully. The most recent number I've seen is 42% of auction listings posted on eBay sell successfully.

Hopefully, the number you get will be somewhere north of 50%.

Now it's time to dig deeper into the items that sold.

- Were they listed as an auction or fixed price?
- What was the high and low selling price?
- What was the average selling price?
- Did the auction listing use buy it now? If so, how many buyers used buy it now to purchase the item?
- Did the fixed price listing use best offer? If so, how many buyers used it to buy the item?
- What prices did sellers start their auction listings at?
- How many pictures did sellers use in their listings?
- What keywords did sellers use in their titles? What keywords did sellers use in their descriptions?
- How was the item description worded? Did the seller use bullet points? Lots of white space? Or, lots of description?
- Did the seller offer free shipping?
- Did the seller use flat rate or calculated shipping?
- What was the average shipping price?

These are just a few of the questions you should ask yourself as you research your market. The more information you have, the easier it will be to pick items that sell and craft superior item descriptions.

The next thing you want to do is check out your competition.

If you followed through with the exercise listed above, you should have discovered some sellers in your potential niche. Run another advanced search for an item you are considering selling.

Visit the seller's eBay store.

Check out the design first. Does the seller have a custom storefront? Do they have a custom listing header with categories and search features? Do they have store categories set up (usually, there's a category list to the left of the store items)? Are they using promotional boxes to feature their items or shipping rates?

This is going to give you some good general information and help you to understand what you're up against. Take a look at how much feedback each seller has, and record the names of the top five sellers. You may even want to sign up for their store newsletters. This will help you do some strategic spying on your competitors.

When you are finished looking at the store, click into some of the categories and see what items sellers are offering. How broad is their product line? Do they sell at the low or high end of the price spectrum? And, finally—how many items are listed in their store?

It's a lot of information to digest, but by the time you are done, you will know a lot about your competition.

The next part of your plan is to put it all together. Examine what your top three to five competitors are doing. Look at their price, their shipping charges, their product line, and the way their items are listed.

Ask yourself –

1. What products aren't they offering that buyers in that niche would want?
2. What products, services, or features can you add to the mix that would make you stand out compared to these sellers?
3. Do you want to compete on price? Service? A broader product line?
4. What shipping strategy do you need to use—free? Low price? Etc.?
5. What tone do you need to set in your listings to attract buyers away from your competitors? Do you need to be serious, humorous, or just offer a more complete listing?

It's a lot of work, but if you do it all, you are going to know your competition and what it's going to take to attract buyers to your eBay listings.

Uncover Your Niche

The real key to success on eBay today is to cultivate a niche and carefully grow it by adding a steady stream of new products.

A lot of people get started selling on eBay by selling everything but the kitchen sink. They sell spare items they find around the house. Then, they begin selling items they find at garage sales, yard sales, and estate sales. Sometimes, it works, but it's a tough sell because it's hard to get repeat customers when you sell a mish-mash of stuff.

To be successful, you need to build your tribe of fanatical customers who keep returning to your eBay store to see what's next? You need them to keep asking themselves, what crazy or unique item did this guy find now?

If you can develop even one hundred regular customers who check back every week or every month, you will be successful selling on eBay.

....

The definition of a niche is a subset or small portion of a larger market.

For example—clothing isn't a niche. Women's clothing isn't a niche. Plus-sized women's work suits or plus-sized women's swimwear is a niche.

Books aren't a niche. Books about Western Americana are a very general niche. Antiquarian books about Western bad men are a niche, as are vintage illustrated children's books.

Ideally, your niche should be in an area you enjoy and have at least some knowledge of. You're going to be spending a lot of time with it. The more you know about your niche, the products in it, and how to determine their condition, the easier it's going to be to source and sell products.

....

When I first jumped into the eBay selling game, I was all over the place. I tossed up some old clothes, random household stuff – you name it. But then, I got into a groove. I started specializing in DVDs, VHS movies, and vintage sports cards from the '50s and '60s.

I made some sales and even had a few folks coming back for more, but honestly, the cash wasn't exactly flooding in. You see, I was snagging those movies online in bulk, like 100 or 500-case loads. Many of those flicks were just going for a couple of bucks, and I was buying them for a buck a pop, so, yeah, I was scraping together a few bucks here and there. After a couple of months, I'd bundle up the movies that weren't flying off the shelf and sell 'em in packs of 25, 50, or 100, starting at just 50 cents each. That way, I could at least break even on the less popular ones or maybe make a few pennies.

Then, it hit me — the movie market on eBay was huge but also pretty cutthroat. So, I had to pivot.

Now, sports cards, that was another story. I was making sales, especially with those '50s and '60s baseball cards and a sprinkling of football ones. I didn't have any secret sauce or anything. I'd snag "lots" and "partial" sets from eBay and Yahoo, break 'em apart, and sell the individual cards for a buck or maybe ten. Every few months, I'd bundle up the cards that just wouldn't budge into packs by team or year.

Sure, I wasn't scoring any home runs, and I couldn't exactly call it a full-time gig, but it was more like a hobby that brought in some extra dough.

But then, I hit a wall. I didn't have the big bucks to move into the high-value cards, and I didn't want to stay in the basement forever. So, I cut ties, cleared out my stash, and ventured into something new.

....

Around that time, I stumbled upon this guy selling magazine articles on eBay. It might've sounded a bit crazy, but I kept my eye on his listings for a while, and he was making some decent sales. Nothing to make you scream, but it got me thinking maybe there was room to take it up a notch.

I did some eBay snooping to see if anyone else was doing the same thing, and he pretty much had the market on lockdown back then. A few sellers were into vintage magazine ads and prints, and a couple were peddling old car literature, ads, and service manuals.

But what I saw made me think, "Hey, there's something here." So, I snagged an 1865 *Harper's New Monthly Magazine* for fifteen bucks and dove in. That $15 turned into $250, and over the next year, it snowballed into over $10,000 in sales.

Turned out, without me realizing it for a while, I'd stumbled into a pretty profitable niche. Fast forward a few years, I was in a job interview at a car dealership. After chatting about what I did on eBay, the sales manager came out with, "You stole that idea, didn't you?" I just nodded, curious about where he was headed with this.

"It's cool," he said, "the best ideas are the ones we borrow."

He had a point. Yeah, I borrowed the idea, but I polished it and turned it into my thing by focusing on history, biography, and science. Over time, I tossed in vintage prints, War of 1812 newspapers, and Spanish-American War prints.

My niche was a work in progress. It still is, always changing based on what my customers want and the cool stuff I come across. These days, old magazine articles and prints have taken a backseat to pop culture memorabilia. It wasn't my original plan, but it's what folks want, so I'm shifting my product lineup to keep 'em happy.

And that's how my eBay journey began. Fast forward half a million dollars in sales later, and things are starting to unravel. The economy is part of the problem. My biggest buyers, like universities, museums, and libraries, saw their funds dry up post-2008. Changes in the eBay platform didn't help, especially the shift away from auction listings. Most of my stuff became nearly invisible in searches, with all those fixed-price listings flooding the place.

A smart seller would've called it quits ages ago, but not me. I kept patching up my brand, trying to breathe new life into it.

It's still pulling in a couple of grand a month, but let's face it, the writing's on the wall. Next year, I'm gonna be diving into a fresher, more profitable niche.

....

Here are a couple of pointers to help you pinpoint your niche:

Take It Easy. Sometimes, your ideal niche can come your way, just like it did for me. Keep an eye on what's selling like hotcakes on eBay, Amazon, and other online shops. Stay updated with the latest happenings by watching the news, catching TV shows, or reading blogs and your local newspaper.

But here's a sneaky trick: just observe the folks around you. Plop down in a mall's food court, eavesdrop on conversations, and see which shops people flock to and which ones they steer clear of. Pay attention to what they're wearing, especially the younger crowd. New trends are always popping up; you just need to have your radar on.

Most of us don't spot trends until they're practically part of our daily lives. That's why only a few lucky souls struck gold with companies like Microsoft, Apple, or AOL. Trends sneak up on us. They start off hidden and then turn into everyday stuff. A niche is a bit like a new trend – it's right there under your nose every day, just tricky to see until you open your eyes wide and let it in.

Size Matters. Your niche needs to have enough potential customers to keep you busy and rake in the income you're after. If it's too narrow or super specialized, you'll run out of folks to sell to.

Here's an example: When I was a new eBay seller, a guy was hawking back issues of various publications from the State Historical Society of Iowa. He was making a nice $15 to $30 per issue and selling ten to fifteen every week. Not too shabby. But I dug a bit deeper and found out that the State Historical Society had a boatload of issues, and they'd hand 'em over at 50¢ or $1.00 a pop. Sweet profit margin, right?

But the potential was quite limited. The market for Iowa history on eBay was just too small. It was perfect for that one guy to pull in some part-time cash, but it wouldn't fly on a bigger scale... unless I took action. So, I reached out to nearly every historical society in the United States to ask about their back-issue prices.

Here's the scoop: it would've been nearly impossible to make it work. A few states, like Missouri and Wyoming, offered back issues at prices close to Iowa's. But most states wanted at least $5.00 a pop. Some, like California, realized the goldmine they were sitting on and slapped on prices of $10.00, $20.00, or even more per copy. That sealed the deal – not profitable enough to build a real business.

So, remember this as you search for your niche. The sooner you figure out it's a dud, the more time and cash you'll save.

Having a steady stream of new products ready to roll is absolutely crucial for your growth. You might have your eyes on the hottest niche around, but if you can't lay your hands on enough products to keep the wheels turning, you're in for a bumpy ride. If you sell vintage stuff, you need to ensure there's a consistent supply available. If you're all about handmade crafts, ask yourself if you can whip up enough goodies to make it worthwhile. And if you're sourcing your goods from a wholesaler, you better crunch those numbers to make sure you can cover your costs and still rake in a decent profit.

Don't just look at the initial cost; take a good, hard look at the shipping expenses both to you and your end customers. And don't forget to think about how flexible your pricing can be. When you first dive into selling a fresh product, you might be the lone ranger or have just a handful of competitors. But as your niche heats up, more sellers are bound to join the party.

Here's a hiccup I ran into. My inventory cost me next to nothing, but thanks to the sheer number of listings I had to maintain on eBay, my fees went through the roof. eBay fees could easily tack on an extra $8.00 to $10.00 to an item that costs me 25 cents or less.

Every few months, new sellers would pop up, thinking they could undercut me by selling the same stuff for $5.00 or $10.00, assuming they could make a quick buck. The harsh reality? They'd last three to six months and then vanish from eBay.

So, the bottom line is you've got to keep that pipeline of products flowing, and you need to be able to sell them at a price that actually makes you money, or else, well, you won't be able to keep the show running.

A lot of eBay sellers swear by the idea of cornering the market on their niche to thrive on the platform, but I'm not entirely sold on that notion. If you find no competition for the products you want to sell, it could mean two things. It's either a brand-new, never-before-seen product, or there's simply no demand for it, and other sellers have tried and thrown in the towel.

When you research a market and find no one else peddling the same products, it's time for some soul-searching. There could be reasons for this scarcity. Maybe the supply of these products is limited, or the demand is practically non-existent. Perhaps it's so new that most people have no idea what it is, or it's just a logistical nightmare to ship or too pricey.

Before you dive headfirst into a niche, do your homework thoroughly and ensure you're clear on what you're getting yourself into. Remember, you're going to be in a long-term relationship with that product line.

Start small. Dip your toes in the water. Sell a few products and test out the waters before you go all in. It's a smart way to figure out if you and your chosen niche are a good match.

Here's another important nugget of wisdom: Make sure your niche has enough breathing room for growth, allowing you to bring in new products over time.

Take my journey, for instance. I kicked off my eBay gig selling magazine articles. As time rolled on, I mixed in prints, vintage newspapers, and various paper treasures. I even took the leap a few times, creating niche stores dedicated to rock 'n roll and sports memorabilia.

Your chosen niche should be wide enough to welcome new products and opportunities to branch out into fresh markets. Don't be afraid to experiment with new items. If they start flying off the shelves, think about setting up a brand-new eBay store catering to that specific niche.

Finding and developing a niche isn't a cakewalk, but it's the most profitable route on eBay. When you've nailed it, you won't have to go hunting for customers; they'll come knocking on your digital storefront.

Ship Like a Pro

*(Much of this section was originally published in my book - **eBay Shipping Simplified**. It's a primer on shipping, packing, and fees. The information in this section can save you thousands of dollars every year.)*

U nderstanding how to ship the items you sell is just as important as knowing which items to sell.

Online sellers face two types of shipping situations: domestic (shipping within your home country) and international (shipping outside of your home country). Many sellers spend years trying their hardest to avoid making international sales because they're afraid of the extra paperwork involved or that there may be excessive damage claims, theft, or negative feedback caused by shipping or communication glitches.

The truth is international shipping is no more difficult than domestic shipping. It's just a matter of learning and getting used to the extra paperwork involved.

Domestic Shipping

Most of the shipping you are going to do is considered domestic shipping or shipping within your home country.

The Post Office offers many ways to ship items. The shipping method you choose depends on the item you are shipping, its size, value, and how quickly you want it to arrive.

Here is a breakdown of the most common shipping services available from the post office and the different items you can ship with them.

- **Media mail** is designed to ship books, CDs, DVDs, and other educational materials. Media mail does have a few restrictions. The material cannot contain any advertising pages, so most magazines are ineligible for media mail shipping. eBay stopped offering media mail as an option for magazine sales in 2023, so sellers skirting postal regulations were forced to follow the rules. As a result, costs went up for buyers and sellers.

  Packages sent by media mail are subject to inspection by the Post Office, so if you do include ineligible items, they can send the items back to you postage due. The main advantage to sellers from using media mail is it's cheaper to ship heavier items like books. As a result, you can offer your customers a less expensive delivery option. This is especially important if you are selling in the book category.

  Delivery time is normally 3 to 8 business days, but can vary based on the season. At Christmas time, it can take as long as two to three weeks to deliver a media mail package, so be sure to give buyers a heads up – "Hey. It's cheap, but it's slow." That way, they understand it's the post office, not you.

- **USPS Ground Advantage**. First-class shipping transitioned to Ground Advantage in 2023. For most sellers, it was a simple change. If you ship smaller items (less than 13 oz.), first class is going to be the most economical method available. You can ship just about anything—books, clothes, DVDs, CDs, jewelry, stamps, postcards, you name it. Tracking is not available on all Ground Advantage packages, so you cannot offer proof of delivery.

  If you are mailing flat items like baseball cards and postcards, then you cannot add tracking. Your package is required to be a minimum of 1/8" thick. Delivery time is normally 1 to 3 days, depending on where you are sending your package. The biggest advantage of the new service is it includes $100 insurance at no additional cost.

- **eBay Standard Envelope**. In 2021, eBay introduced a new shipping service called eBay Standard Envelope. It's a way for sports card sellers to offer low-cost tracking on items valued under $20. Again, the cost is reasonable—between 57 cents and $1.05, compared to big dollars for priority shipping. A one-ounce package is 57 cents, a two-ounce package is 81 cents, and a three-ounce parcel is $1.05. But keep in mind prices are likely to change as the post office refines the service.

eBay Standard Envelope comes with many restrictions. You can read more here. https://pages.ebay.com/ebaystandardenvelope/index.html.

Currently, the service is off to a bumpy start. E-Commerce Bytes blog reports many sellers say tracking is nonexistent, most likely because postal employees aren't scanning the packages. Service could improve as postal employees become more aware of it. But, for now, beware and ship at your own risk.

eBay says they are expanding the service for sellers in low-value categories where tracking is not cost-effective. Let's hope they eliminate the bugs before moving forward.

- **Priority Mail**. The majority of items sold by online sellers ship by priority mail. It has several advantages over other services, including:
1) You can mail heavier items than first class,
2) Most items deliver within 1 to 3 days, and
3) Tracking is available for all packages, so you have proof of delivery for eBay and your customers, and

4) The Post Office provides free shipping materials, so you don't have to invest in boxes and other expensive packaging materials.

5) You can schedule a pickup, and the post office will send a carrier to your home or business to pick up your packages.

The disadvantage to using priority mail is that it is more expensive than first class or media mail.

- **Priority Mail Flat Rate** takes the guesswork out of shipping. You can ship whatever will fit in the package, regardless of the weight, anywhere in the United States for a preset fee. This is a great option for buyers and sellers because it's less expensive to ship heavier items or multiple items that will fit into a single package.

  Like regular priority mail—it's quick, offers 1 to 3-day delivery, comes with delivery confirmation, and packaging materials are free from the Post Office. Be sure you use the Flat Rate Priority Mail boxes when using this service.

- **Standard Post** is a less expensive option for mailing parcels and oversized packages. The normal delivery time is 2 to 8 business days. Tracking is included in your shipping fees.

- **Express Mail** offers overnight delivery service to most areas in the United States. If your customer needs an item quick, this is the service for them. Be aware it's expensive, and the fees depend on the size and weight of the package you are sending.

  Like Priority Mail, Express Mail offers free packaging materials and delivery confirmation. Sellers also receive $100 of insurance free with most parcels sent and signature delivery confirmation, which eBay and PayPal require on more expensive packages.

- **Priority Mail Express Flat Rate** offers next-day delivery (in most areas), plus the added convenience of simplified rates. When you use the flat rate boxes, anything you mail in them (regardless of weight) ships for one fee, so if you're shipping heavy items—this is the service for you.

To get the full scoop on these delivery services, check out the following link. https://www.usps.com/ship/compare-domestic-services.htm

Package Your Items Like a Pro

How you package the items you sell makes a major difference in how buyers view you as a seller.

If you just toss your items into a box or envelope, it's going to leave a sour taste in the minds of your buyers. Their purchases are likely to arrive damaged or with bumped and scuffed-up packaging that looks like it's been run through the wringer.

I know many books recommend recycling used boxes, packing materials, and such to use for your shipping. In my mind—that's the worst mistake you can make.

You only get one chance to make a good first impression. If your package arrives, all scuffed up or with all sorts of squiggly lines where you crossed out previous addresses, customers will be concerned about their purchases. If that's the way you package stuff, your buyers will think, "God help me" about the stuff you put inside the box.

Set Up Your Shipping Station

Most sellers, I've worked with ship their items from the same desk they sell from. If you're a part-time seller, that's okay. If you eBay for a living, I'd recommend a separate shipping station.

Here's why.

Shipping is a specialized task. To do it right, you need a lot of space and all of your packaging materials and supplies nearby. I have a separate desk and table set up for shipping. I only use my shipping computer when I'm shipping items or tracking shipments. It's an older castoff, but it serves the purpose. I have two printers hooked up to it...a Zebra LP 2844 and a Samsung laser printer.

Most of my shipping labels get printed on the Zebra. I use the laser printer to print packing slips and thank you cards. I also have a postal scale that attaches to the computer through the USB port. It's digital and can accurately weigh up to twenty-five pounds in one-ounce increments. The weight automatically gets transferred into Stamps.com with one click of my mouse, so there's never any guesswork involved. I normally round up to the next ounce to add a little wiggle room for tape or the label.

I have sturdy warehouse shelving set up opposite my desk. The bottom row has flat boxes in various sizes. The next shelf has priority mailboxes and envelopes. The shelf above that has stay-flat mailers and padded mailers. The top shelf has all of my miscellaneous supplies—shipping labels, paper, extra rolls of tape, box cutters, and Sharpie markers.

Everything is nearby. Once I get started, I can normally package and ship thirty or forty items in an hour. Before I had my shipping station, it took twice as long because I was running from here to there looking for stuff or trying to find a good spot to spread all my stuff out.

Must-Have Supplies

There are certain equipment and supplies you need to keep on hand so you can ship smart.

>> Packaging material. Stock up on boxes, padded mailers, stay-flat mailers, bubble wrap, and tape. The worst thing that can happen is to be in the middle of packaging up your orders and then discover you don't have the supplies you need.

If you ship priority or express mail, stop by the post office and pick up the supplies you need. Better yet, hop online and check out https://store.usps.com/store/browse/category.jsp?categoryId=shipping-supplies. Order your boxes ten, twenty-five, or more at a time, depending on how quick you go through them. The post office will deliver them free within two to three days.

If you need to purchase boxes, padded mailers, or stay-flat mailers—consider Uline - http://www.uline.com/. They have decent prices and quick delivery.

Wal-Mart carries a great selection of boxes in its shipping supply aisle. The prices are good, especially when you compare them to the big box office supply stores.

I've also had good luck buying supplies from several suppliers on eBay.

. Value Mailers
http://stores.ebay.com/VALUEMAILERS?_trksid=p2047675.l2563

. Royal Mailers
http://stores.ebay.com/Royalmailers?_trksid=p2047675.l2563

>> **Postal scale**. If you sell online, you need a postal scale. I know a lot of sellers try to fudge it and just guess at weights. Trust me. No one is that good. Every ounce you guess wrong costs you at least seventeen cents. Over a year, that will cost you one hundred dollars or more.

Best advice: buy a good digital scale. You can find scales with weight capacities starting at five pounds.

>> **Printer**. The printer you use is a matter of preference. I like to use a Zebra label printer because it prints a small compact label you can peel off and stick on your package. There's no messing with tape or ink cartridges because it's a thermal printer. The next best choice is a laser printer. The ink is less expensive, and it prints quicker. There's nothing more aggravating than waiting for a slow inkjet printer to finish printing your label. The last choice is an inkjet printer. It's slow, but it will get the job done. If you use adhesive-backed labels, an inkjet printer is your best bet. Whenever I tried them in my laser printer, they were too thick and jammed it up.

>> **Shipping tape**. I usually pick up my tape at SAMs Club or Walmart. You can buy single rolls or save a few bucks and buy

them in six packs. My only recommendation is not to buy the cheapest tape you can find. It tears, it splits, and it's a mess restarting the roll.

>> **Bubble wrap**. If you are packaging china, old books, or other fragile items, you're going to need bubble wrap. Here's one item it's okay to reuse. Good places to purchase bubble wrap are SAMs Club, Walmart, or online.

>> **Box cutter**. Be sure to keep a couple of box cutters and plenty of extra razor blades on hand. You want to package your items right, and the best way to do that is to give everything a snug, tight fit. To do that, you need a box cutter with a sharp blade so you can easily refit boxes.

>> **Peanuts** are those little white foam half-circles shippers use to line their packages. They are all static-filled and stick to everything. I hate them and refuse to buy anything else from sellers that use them. Use peanuts at your risk; they are a sticky mess.

If you have an eBay store, be sure to take advantage of the free shipping supplies they offer. Every quarter, sellers receive $50 to $150 credit towards boxes, packing tape, and other assorted supplies.

Packaging Tips

O kay. You set up your shipping station and stocked up on supplies. Now it's time for *Packaging 101*.

The best tip I can give you is always to choose the right type of packaging and err on the side of more packing materials, not less. Don't skimp on packing materials. It will come back to haunt you.

Tip #1. Choose the right type of packaging. If you are shipping a newer book or a paperback, it's okay to use a padded mailer. If you are shipping a rare book or vintage book, you need to package it differently. Use a box and make sure to place it inside a sealed plastic bag, and then wrap it with newspaper or bubble wrap. Doing this keeps the corners from getting scuffed or bent, and it protects the book from moisture damage should your box be exposed to water.

If you are shipping china, glass figurines, or other fragile materials, pick a box about six inches larger all around than what you are shipping. Line the box with bubble wrap or wadded-up newspapers. Next, wrap each item in bubble wrap or newspaper and tape it up so it is secure. Lay the item in the box and cover it with bubble wrap or newspaper. Continue doing this until the box is full. Build another layer of bubble wrap or wadded-up newspapers at the top. You will know you've got it right when you shake the box. If something shifts or rattles inside, add more packing material.

When you ship electronics, laptops, or tablets, your best bet is to ship them in the original box. If that isn't possible, find a box just slightly larger than the item you're going to ship. Build a nest in the box using foam, bubble wrap, or wadded-up newspapers. Place your item in a sealed plastic bag to prevent moisture damage. Wrap it several times with bubble wrap. Place the item in the box. Wrap any accessories, discs, power cord, etc. separately and place them in the box. Build a nest around the top of the box before you seal it to ensure the item won't get damaged in transit. Tape all of the way around the circumference of the box, length-wise and width-wise. Doing this ensures the tape won't break free where the box can come open in shipment.

If you are shipping clothes, you can pop a shirt or t-shirt into a priority mail bag. If you are shipping jackets, jeans, or multiple items, use a flat rate priority mail box to reduce your costs. If you are unsure which is cheaper—regular priority mail or flat rate, weigh it out and let the numbers do the talking.

I'm not going to describe any more scenarios. Just understand that you need to adapt every packing situation to the item you are shipping.

I have received close to a thousand packages over the last twenty years. Some of them were perfectly packed, some were adequate, and quite a few arrived banged up and had the items I purchased hanging halfway out of the box or missing.

Tip #2. The best time to decide how to pack an item for shipment is before you list it.

Think about it. If you list a computer or rare figurine—how are you going to determine shipping charges if you don't know how you're going to pack and ship it?

In my case, I have hundreds of rare newspapers dating from 1806 to the Civil War period, but I don't have a cost-effective method to ship individual papers. If I fold the paper to make the size manageable, I will ruin a good part of the item's collectability. To ship a single paper would require me to buy an oversized casing for it and then a custom box to put it in. Packaging could easily run forty to fifty dollars before shipping costs. That's a hefty chunk of change to add to a paper I'm selling for twenty-five dollars.

The economics don't work out in this case, so the papers remain in my private collection for now.

Make sure you are not going to go underwater on the items you sell. Before you list an item, determine what it's going to take to ship it. What kind of packaging materials do you need? How much is shipping likely to cost? Is the item expensive enough to require insurance? If so, how much is that going to cost?

Know what you are looking at upfront because, after the sale, you can't come back and ask the buyer for more money.

A lot of sellers box their items up at the time they list them. They weigh the package and input the weight into the eBay shipping calculator. When the item sells, they grab the box, print a label, and drop it in the mail.

Do whatever works for you.

Just keep in mind buyers always have questions. You may need to open the box up to answer a question or to shoot a quick picture or two. Also, not every item sells. You may need to bundle that item up with several other items to make a sale.

Do I Need to Offer Free Shipping?

Free shipping is the biggest bugaboo confronting online sellers right now.

eBay encourages sellers to offer free shipping, and they promote items with free shipping to buyers. Because of this, many new sellers think they must offer free shipping. Let me assure you: that's not true.

You don't have to offer free shipping on any of the items you sell. However, you may want to offer free shipping. Here's why?

Normally, sales increase when you offer free shipping. There's something about "free" and "shipping" that makes buyers loosen up their purse strings and spend more money. I'm not sure what it is, but the word "free" is one of those magical keys that can get consumers to pull the trigger and spend more money.

Keep that info tucked away in the back of your head for a moment.

Just because eBay likes free shipping and consumers like free shipping doesn't mean it's the magical ingredient you have been searching for to increase your sales and profits. It needs to be the right combination that's good for both of you. That means you need to be able to make a profit, and your customer needs to get a good value when you offer free shipping.

How does that work?

If you sell lightweight, easy-to-ship items, free shipping should be a no-brainer. Let me repeat that. If you sell light items, you can ship in an envelope or padded mailer and ship for under a dollar; you are probably better off giving your customers free shipping rather than trying to charge them that buck. So, if you sell postcards, baseball cards, small knickknacks, and inexpensive jewelry items that you mail in a regular envelope—mark your item up a buck and give your customer free shipping.

If you are selling heavier items, low-margin items, or custom-made items, free shipping may make sense. Before you pull the trigger, though, do your research. Investigate what other sellers with similar items are doing. If everyone else offers free shipping, you will be better off following the pack, unless...and, this is a big unless. If everyone else has marked their item up enough to cover shipping, plus a couple of extra bucks for profit, it might make sense to charge shipping and price your item as low as you can while still holding a decent profit.

If some sellers in your category offer free shipping and some charge for shipping, you may want to test the waters. Offer a few items with free shipping and a few with your regular shipping charges. Run with the method that makes the most sales for you.

If you are the only one selling a certain product and you are making a killer profit, go ahead and give your customers free shipping. It's like extra icing on the cake. It's one more reason to buy from you.

Setting Shipping Rates on eBay

S etting shipping rates is another tricky area that can confuse sellers.

Here's the least you need to know.

- If you're a Top-Rated Seller or want to be a Top-Rated Seller, you are required to provide tracking information for all of your domestic sales. You are also required to post tracking information back into the listing on a minimum of 90% of the items you sell.
- Top-rated sellers are required to ship all of their items with a one-day handling period.
- If the value of any item you sell is over $200, you are required to provide signature delivery confirmation.

If you're not a Top-Rated Seller and don't have any intention of becoming one, it's still a good idea to provide delivery confirmation on every item you send. It protects you from bad buyers who may open an item not received case because they know they will win if you can't provide proof of delivery.

Now, we will get down to the nitty-gritty of setting up shipping in your item listings.

To set your domestic shipping options, look for the section labeled *add shipping details* on your sell your item form.

The first choice you need to make is to select your shipping method from the drop-down box. There are four possible choices: flat cost, calculated, freight, and no shipping—local pickup. Flat cost is where you charge all buyers the same shipping rate. Calculated shipping uses the eBay shipping calculator to figure shipping based on your item weight and its destination. Freight is for larger items too big to ship by the USPS or UPS. Items shipping by freight are carried by a semi or common carrier.

If you sell large items that need to ship by a common carrier, keep in mind eBay's freight calculator only works up to 150 pounds. If your item exceeds 150 pounds, you need to use flat-rate shipping. You also need to understand how truck lines work. Most carriers only require their drivers to pull your item to the back of the truck. It's up to your customers to have people available to help them get their items out of the truck and carry them inside the house.

You need to explain this to your customers in your listing description and again in the shipping instructions you send the buyer after the sale. Here's another tip. You can request the truck line to call your customer the day before delivery. Sometimes, they will do it; sometimes, they won't, so try not to make too many promises.

To set up calculated shipping, click the blue lettering that says *calculate shipping*. A pop-up box will open up. Fill in the options, and you're good to go.

If you use flat-rate shipping, click on the box that says standard shipping. Select the shipping service you want to set up and enter the shipping fee in the smaller box to the right where it says cost. If you want to offer free shipping for that service, put a checkmark where it says free shipping. To offer more shipping options, click the blue lettering that says *offer additional service*.

To offer local pickup, check the box where it says *Local Pickup*. Be careful when you select this option because local pickup is not available in all categories.

Think long and hard before you offer local pickup for your items. Do you really want to invite customers into your home? Over the years, I've had some local buyers insist on picking up their items to save on shipping. Most times, I've delivered the items to their business or met the customer outside of McDonald's or another local business. It's less risky but a major pain in the backside.

Best advice: avoid local pickup whenever possible.

If you set up flat shipping rules, you can check the box to apply them. If you would like to set up or edit your rules, click on the blue lettering that says *edit rules*. The pop-up box will walk you through setting up shipping discounts. If you edit the top set of rules, the changes are only good for the listing you are currently working on. If you want to create a discount for all of your listings, you need to scroll down to the bottom of the pop-up box where it says Promotional Shipping Rule (applies to all items).

If you haven't used this feature before, you should give it a whirl. You would be surprised how many buyers will shop for additional items to save a few bucks on shipping.

The next choice you have is to select the *handling time*. If you are a Top-Rated Seller, you are required to ship all items within one day, so be sure to select that option.

The final item gives you a nudge to add next-day shipping to your listing. I don't offer the service unless buyers contact me and say they have to have next-day shipping. My reason for not offering next-day shipping is very few people request it, and you have deadlines you need to meet to get the item to the post office on time. It takes more effort than it's worth.

That's it. Your shipping options are done.

Here's another quick tip so you don't have to go through this with every item you list—set up one of your listings as a template, or when you list new items, pull up one of your old listings and select the option to sell a similar item. When you use either of these options, your previous info transfers over to the new listings. Use the info you want to keep, type over, or delete the unwanted info.

Printing Shipping Labels Using eBay

eBay lets sellers print shipping labels directly from its site. The process is easy to use and lets you print professional-looking labels and invoices to include with your shipments.

Print eBay Shipping Labels

The easiest way to print shipping labels using eBay is to go into your *Selling Manager*. In the left-hand column, find where it says *Selling Manager Pro*. Just down from there, you will see the word *sold*. Select it.

That's going to bring up a list of your sold items. Locate the item you want to ship, and scroll over to the far right column labeled actions. The first thing you should see is *Print Shipping*.

When you select *Print Shipping,* it takes you to the eBay ship your item page. When you click on it, the page prepopulates with all of your item information.

At the top of the page, it shows the item description, the price paid, the shipping fee, the shipping service paid for, and the expected delivery date. The left-hand column contains the shipping information—the buyer's address and your address. If you need to change the address, select where it says change and enter the correct shipping information.

Just below the address details, you will see a box labeled Add Message to buyer email. I have a standard thank you message in here, but you can use it to tell your buyer a little more about the item or direct them to your store specials. It's up to you.

The center column contains the package details. It's where you choose the carrier, add shipping options, and choose your mailing date. eBay has two approved carriers: the United States Postal Service (USPS) and FedEx. My shipping experience has all been with the USPS, so that's what I'm going to cover here. If you ship using FedEx, select them as the carrier and follow the prompts to complete your shipment.

The first thing you need to do is select your carrier. In this case, choose USPS.

Use the next box to select your shipping service. The choices are priority mail, first class package, parcel select, media mail, and priority mail express. The priority mail and priority mail express options let you choose the level of service you want.

After you've selected your service, you have the option of printing the auction number or some other message on the label. Check the box and type in your message. The default message is the auction ID.

You select the mailing date in the final box. The choices are today, tomorrow, or the next day. The reason for this is you are supposed to mail your package the same day you print the label, so if you are printing the label today but not mailing your package for two days, you should change the date. I have never had a problem with the post office if I'm a day or two late dropping the package in the mail, but your local post office may see things differently.

The third column shows your postage cost broken down by the postage cost, the delivery confirmation fee, and the total cost. Below that, you have the option to hide the shipping so buyers can't see how much actual shipping costs you. It's your choice—if you are playing by the rules and charging actual shipping, let your buyers see the shipping cost. It will prove you're on the up-and-up.

Click purchase postage, and your account gets charged the shipping fees. The next screen shows a mockup of the label. You can print a sample or print the label.

After the label prints, the program will automatically transfer tracking information into the item listing so buyers can follow the movement of their package.

Do I Need Insurance?

W hen eBay allowed sellers to charge customers for insurance, I required all my buyers to purchase it. It saved a lot of hassles. If the item got lost, the customer received a refund.

What I discovered after shipping over 40,000 items is very few items get lost, stolen, or damaged in transit. I think I have had two damaged packages and three lost packages in twenty-five years. So, is insurance necessary? It depends on you and your tolerance for loss. Most of the items I ship cost between twenty to twenty-five dollars. Insurance costs close to two bucks for each package. Take two bucks times forty thousand packages, and that's close to eighty thousand dollars.

My losses in all this time have amounted to under one hundred bucks. If I'd bought insurance on every item I shipped, I'd be out close to $60,000. When you look at it that way—insurance doesn't make sense.

But...insuring my more expensive packages does make me feel all warm and fuzzy inside. Because of that, I picked a number where I would insure my shipments. If the value exceeds that number, I purchase insurance. For me, the magic number is fifty dollars. For you, it may be ten dollars or one hundred dollars. The best I can tell you is to choose your threshold for loss and make a decision to insure all shipments that exceed that number—that way, you can sleep nights. If you ship everything by Ground Advantage or Priority Mail, $100 of insurance is included at no additional cost.

Here's the least you need to know about insurance.

- eBay no longer allows sellers to charge buyers for insurance. You can roll it into your shipping costs or bury it in the cost of your item.
- Filing an insurance claim with the Post Office is a pain in the rear end. It takes a minimum of thirty days for the post office to reimburse you. Many times, it can take two or three times that long.
- When you sell something on eBay, it's hard to prove the actual value of an item, especially for collectibles and one-of-a-kind items. Just because you paid five bazillion dollars for a rare candy bar wrapper doesn't mean that's the value of your item.
- You may have insurance, but your customer doesn't care about that. They don't want to wait thirty days or more to get their money back. If you make them wait for a refund, odds are you're going to receive negative feedback.

With all of that said, how do you file an insurance claim? The easiest way is to do it online. Go to the following link: https://www.usps.com/ship/file-domestic-claims.htm. It will walk you through filing an insurance claim for a lost parcel.

Here are a few of the highlights to keep in mind.

You need to upload tracking info for the item, a copy of the sales receipt or your eBay auction listing number (to prove value), and your insurance receipt. If you received a damaged item—you need to save the item, along with all packaging materials, until the claim finishes processing.

If, for some reason, you can't file the online claim, call (800) 275-8777, and they will send you a claim form.

Sell International

Here's a secret many online sellers don't know. The fastest-growing sellers on eBay are powering that growth with international sales. According to a recent article on Linnworks, "76% of [the] fastest growers are primarily trading across borders."

The beauty of selling internationally is when the domestic economy slows down, and sales in your country become sluggish, there are still pockets of growth and increasing demand in foreign economies. The key to tapping into these growth pockets is to make your items available to sellers in those countries.

I started listing items internationally in 2001, and within a year, thirty to thirty-five percent of my orders were shipping overseas. Over the last twenty years, I completed nearly 5,000 international transactions with only two lost packages.

If you are on the line about getting started with international shipping—consider baby-stepping it. Start with proven foreign trade partners like Canada, the United Kingdom, and Australia. There are few language barriers dealing with these countries. You should also consider selling to Germany. According to a recent article in *Forbes Magazine*, Germany and the United Kingdom account for 48 percent of all international sales made on eBay.

....

To qualify for international visibility on eBay, sellers must meet several standards.

- Must have 10 or more positive feedback
- Items must be listed in the appropriate category
- Need to enable shipping to countries you want to ship in
- For best visibility, sellers must specify the levels of shipping service they are offering

The other great thing is if you sell using your eBay.com account, your feedback will be visible to sellers on eBay's foreign sites.

If you are a seller in the United States and specify you will ship to Canada, your items will automatically display on eBay.ca.

Items listed on international sites do not count as duplicate listings, so sellers don't get penalized for listing the same item on different eBay sites.

....

eBay gives you four ways to make your items available to international buyers.

1. Opt into eBay's Global Shipping Program.
2. Enable your items for international shipping.
3. List your items on international sites.

4. Open eBay stores in countries where you do a large amount of business.

Next, I'm going to look at each option in more detail and explain who it is for and how you can get started using it.

eBay Global Shipping Program

S everal years ago, eBay introduced its Global Shipping Program. They revamped the program in the fall of 2022, but most changes are unnoticeable for sellers. The program makes it easy for sellers to jump into international selling without worrying about shipping rules, customs forms, etc.

If you've been itching to start international sales but were afraid of the extra work involved, I suggest giving eBay's Global Shipping Program a shot.

Many small sellers are terrified of international shipping. They've heard so many horror stories about sales going wrong that they're scared to give it a shot. They don't want to fill out customs forms or worry about whether their package will make it to Timbuktu or not.

eBay has eliminated all that grief for sellers. Instead, sellers list their items just like they usually would. Then, when the item sells, they ship it to an eBay shipping center in the United States.

Your responsibility for the shipment is over as soon as it arrives at the shipping center. From that point on, eBay and its shipping partners assume any liability for getting your package to its destination.

Here's how it works.

When you list your item for sale on eBay, check the box to include your item in the Global Shipping Program, and you're ready to go.

Some categories don't qualify for inclusion in the Global Shipping Program. eBay will flag the item and let you know when you bump into these. For example, I do a lot of selling in the collectibles category. Unfortunately, collectibles manufactured before 1899 don't qualify, so I often see this issue pop up. The only way around it is to ship the item internationally yourself.

Sellers can't invoice buyers using the Global Shipping Program when an item sells. eBay takes care of all this for you. The reason is that you cannot know what their shipping fee will be.

Once the customer pays, you receive a payment notice and the shipping address. A simple way to recognize a payment made through the Global Shipping Program is the address will include a long reference number.

Ship your item like you usually would. Include delivery confirmation to ensure the item arrives at the shipping center. Once you have confirmed the item was received, your part in the transaction is complete.

eBay's shipping partner—Pitney Bowes—will readdress the package, fill out all the appropriate customs forms, and ensure delivery to the customer.

That's the way it should happen. But unfortunately, now and then, things don't work out as planned—the customer doesn't receive the item, or it arrives damaged. As a seller, you're supposed to be protected from receiving negative feedback in such a situation. That's right to a point. You need to keep an eye on your feedback profile and keep after eBay to update it should any errors occur.

I received negative feedback due to a customer not receiving their item. I knew it wasn't received because that's what the seller wrote in his feedback. So, I called eBay customer service and explained the problem. After about fifteen minutes of researching the problem, the rep agreed I was not responsible. He removed the negative feedback while we were still on the phone.

If you experience a similar problem, contact eBay customer service immediately. Have the listing item number and the feedback information available and ready to share with them when you call. Make it easy for eBay to help you.

Overall, the Global Shipping Program is an excellent way to increase sales. International sales accounted for roughly thirty-five to forty percent of my eBay sales and profits during my peak selling period.

If you're looking for a simple method to grow your sales, opt into the Global Shipping Program and give it a shot.

Enable Items for International Shipping

W e have already talked about eBay's Global Shipping Program and how easy it is to use, so why would anybody want to ship international packages on their own?

That's a great question.

It comes down to having more control over your shipping options and the ability to make more sales. When you use eBay's Global Shipping Program, they figure in customs fees, a markup to pay themselves and their shipping partner an additional profit, plus actual shipping costs. The final number eBay shows your customer for shipping can be mind-boggling and can cost you the sale.

Let me use the products I sell as an example. When I ship items internationally on my own, I charge $5.00 to ship items to Canada and $9.00 for shipping anywhere else in the world. Sometimes, I make a few extra bucks; sometimes, I lose a few bucks, but over time it averages out. Keep in mind the buyer is still on the line for duty and customs fees when their item arrives.

When I sell the same item using eBay's Global Shipping Program, they charge my customer in the low twenty dollar range for Canada and in the low thirty dollar range for Europe and the rest of the world. My items normally sell for sixteen to twenty-five dollars, so customers are confronted with some serious sticker shock when they see eBay's shipping price.

Self-preservation is one of the major reasons I used to ship international packages myself. With Covid and other issues going on now, I don't know if I'd recommend tackling international shipping on your own.

What I'm going to do now is walk you through setting up the international portion of your eBay sell your item form. It's structured very similar to how you set up your domestic shipping options, so it should be easy to follow along and use.

....

Everything you need to set your international shipping options is located in the box labeled *International Shipping*.

Your first choice is to opt into the Global Shipping Program. In this case, you want to leave that box unchecked.

Below this, you have a drop-down box that offers you the option to select flat rate, calculated shipping, or no additional options. As a quick review, flat rate shipping is where you have one set shipping fee for all buyers. Calculated shipping uses the eBay shipping calculator to determine the shipping price based on the shipping destination. The difference is— flat rate shipping is easier to set up and use, but calculated shipping can give buyers closer to you a break in shipping costs, thus giving you the opportunity to grab additional sales from price-conscious buyers.

After you choose your shipping method, you'll see another drop-down box that says shipping. It gives you three choices:

worldwide, chose a custom location, or Canada. I normally set up a separate price for worldwide and Canada—any more is overkill in my book. However, if you ship a lot of packages to Mexico, the UK, or wherever, go ahead and set up a special price for them, too. The drop-down box next to this lets you choose the type of service you wish to offer, and the box to the right of that lets you set your shipping price.

Below this, you see a line labeled *offer additional service*. You can use this to ship to an additional location or to offer a different delivery method.

In the *additional ship-to locations,* you can check off the areas you are willing to ship to, and the buyer can contact you for more details. Some sellers have lots of rules about where they will and will not ship to. A lot of sellers mark Malaysia, Italy, Mexico, Russia, etc., off limits because it's all over the internet; other people have experienced problems when they ship packages there. In my book, that's all talk. I've shipped items to all those countries and never had a problem. All I'm saying is if you're going to put areas off limits or discourage buyers from certain regions, wait until you have a problem with the area, then evaluate the situation and determine how you want to handle it.

The final line—combined shipping discounts, lets you apply your discount rules to this purchase if you set them up. My items are light and only add a few ounces to the package. Therefore, I ship all additional items for free. It's a great way to encourage buyers to continue shopping with you. If you can't offer to ship all additional items for free—consider offering discounted shipping for additional purchases. It will bring you more business over the long haul.

That's it. You're open for international business. Sit back and wait for the orders to roll in.

I'm going to make one additional suggestion here. Take a few moments to help set buyer expectations. International buyers are similar to domestic buyers—they want to purchase their items today and receive them yesterday.

Most times, shipping goes smoothly, and items arrive on time, but many circumstances are beyond your control, especially when you're dealing with international customers.

I normally post the following information in each of my listings and include it again in my shipping emails.

"Normal international delivery time is eight to fifteen business days, but it can take as long as four to six weeks— depending on customs and other shipping issues. Please be patient and take this into consideration when placing your orders."

It helps to set buyer expectations before buyers place an order. That way, if the customer asks where their item is, you can refer them back to the info posted in your listing. By giving realistic delivery time frames upfront, you're going to save yourself a lot of grief and wasted emails trying to explain why customers haven't received their packages yet.

Remember—International customers have you over the barrel. Tracking is virtually nonexistent for international shipments. The post office is experimenting with international delivery confirmation to select countries, but the service is spotty at best. There's no guarantee the mailman in Canada or the UK will scan your package when he drops it off. He may be having a bad day, or he may be trying to outrun a dog. If your customer decides to file an item not received case, you're going to lose because there's no way to provide proof of delivery.

Sorry to be the one to break it to you, but it's a fact of life when you are doing business on eBay. I've only had this happen once. A buyer in Germany opened an item not received case two days after paying for his item. There was no possible way it could travel from Iowa to Germany in two days.

Guess what? It didn't matter. eBay and PayPal decided the case against me because I didn't have proof of delivery. As I said, this happened in one out of five thousand international shipments, so it's not a big deal.

One other quick comment here—many sellers assume proof of shipping is enough to win an international case. It's not. A stamped customs form from your post office will not help you if the buyer files an item not received case. If you don't have proof of delivery, you don't have a leg to stand on.

List Your Items on International Sites

What we have talked about so far involves listing your items on eBay.com and making them available to buyers in foreign countries. The reason this works is eBay.com is the largest of the eBay sites and has the most listings posted to it. As a result, many international buyers search here first when they're looking for new items.

If you do a lot of business with certain countries, you may be able to increase sales there by listing items directly on that site.

If you are a registered eBay user, you can sell on any of eBay's international sites. To get started, just log in with your current ID and password and start listing your items. Sellers with anchor stores can list on international sites for free. Sellers without an anchor store are charged listing fees if they exceed their free limits.

If you want to make more sales, there are a few details you should consider.

1. What language are you going to post your listings in?

If you're selling in Canada, the United Kingdom, or Australia—English might be fine. But, the UK and Australia use different dialects, and the meanings of words are not always the same. Canada has a large French-speaking population, so you need to consider them, too. Should you post in English and French?

If you post listings in Germany, France, or Japan—what do you do? Many of the buyers there speak English as a second language, but do you want to leave their understanding to chance?

It's a tough call. You can use Google Translate or Bing Translate to write your description. The translations are usually stilted and hard to read. A better choice would be to find a native-language translator on Fiverr or Odesk. They would be able to provide you with a more accurate translation.

If you are selling low-dollar value or one-of-a-kind items, the translation apps are your most cost-effective option. If you're setting up more expensive items you are going to sell over and over again, a good translator can help you create more professional-sounding listings that will make more sales. Look at it as an investment in your success.

Other sellers choose to rely on translation apps that let potential buyers select the language they want to read the description in. eBay offers several of these apps that you can place in your item description. One app is called *One Hour Translation,* and the other is *Translation for Worldwide*.

2. What about your title? Are the keywords and the context the same in German, Spanish, and other languages as they are in the United States?

Do you know what terms someone in Germany would use to search for an iPad or a smartphone? When they're looking for a denim jacket, what other terms would they use to search for it?

Your title is how potential buyers discover your item. If you don't know the local dialect or slang, how do you know the best words to use in your title?

Go back to item one. A translator fluent in the native language would be able to write the most appropriate title for your item listings.

3. What are you going to charge for shipping?

Do you charge international rates, offer free shipping, or split it somewhere in the middle?

Shipping is a key ingredient in determining how successful you'll be at international selling. The good news is items just about always make it to their destination. The bad news is sometimes packages take forever to arrive at their destination.

When I listed items on the eBay.Uk site, I marked my items up a bit and offered free shipping. A funny thing happened— most of my items ended up selling to my regular customers here in the United States. It wasn't quite what I expected, but sales did go up.

After a month, I switched tactics and offered a low-cost international shipping option—five dollars compared to the nine-dollar rate I charged on eBay.com. Once I did that, I started getting more buyers from the U. K.

Joseph Dattilo, the founder of Virtualbotix, LLC, says —

"We offer USPS and UPS shipping providers and generally have First Class International, Priority International, Priority Express International, and UPS International as an option.

Initially, we only had First Class International as an option but found that very few high-value items sold, and we were contacted by dozens of buyers who demanded that we make other methods available.

"Since offering USPS Priority Mail International and USPS Priority Mail Express International, we have seen a dramatic increase in sales of items whose value is greater than $100. The interesting thing is that the boost in sales occurred, but the use of these more expensive services is still rather rare.

The final takeaway is sellers can benefit from offering a larger variety of shipping options, even if their customers decide not to take advantage of them.

4. How are you going to approach delivery time?

Even if you explain your item ships from the United States, many buyers won't understand. All they see is that your item is listed on their home site—eBay.uk or eBay.de.

Shipping time is a tough call with any international shipping method. A lot of my shipments make it to Europe faster than they do across the state. Others seem like they get buried on the proverbial slow boat to China.

The problem is, as a seller, you have no way of knowing which packages are going to get tied up in customs. The best you can do is help to set reliable delivery expectations for your customers.

Offer your customers a variety of mailing options—First Class International, Priority International, and Priority Express International, then give them time frames for delivery using each service. Tell customers the longest it should take for items to be delivered. Most often, their package will arrive sooner, and customers will be delighted because the item was delivered sooner than they expected.

5. Are you going to price your item in U S dollars, Pounds Sterling, or Euros?

If you sell on eBay.uk or eBay.de and price your item in dollars, it's going to confuse buyers. If you price your item in Pounds Sterling or Euros, you need to keep a close eye on currency fluctuations to ensure you don't end up taking a bath if the market turns. When you pull your money out of PayPal, it's a two-step process. You have to convert your currency to U S dollars first and then transfer funds to your bank account.

6. What are you going to tell your customers about VAT taxes, customs fees, and duty fees?

Customers won't understand why they have to pay extra fees and taxes. When you list items on their home site, they don't associate the purchase, triggering additional fees for customs and duty.

To prevent negative feedback and multiple returns, you need to explain in every listing that your item ships from the United States, and customers are responsible for all customs and duty fees as well as VAT taxes. You need to include the same information in every shipping email.

Joseph Dattilo of Virtuabotix says they adhere to eBay's policy on every international listing and include the following disclaimer in every item description –

"For international orders (outside of the United States of America), please allow for additional time for your products to arrive, or choose one of our expedited services to ensure your product arrives in a timely manner. Basic international shipping can take as much as 30 to 60 days, depending on your country, while expedited international shipments have guaranteed delivery windows.

"Import duties, taxes, and charges are not included in the item price or shipping cost. These charges are the buyer's responsibility.

"Please check with your country's customs office to determine what these additional costs will be before bidding or buying."

All sellers should include similar wording in their international listings. If you don't include similar wording, eBay may decide a case against you if a customer opens a buyer protection case against you, citing extended delivery times or additional fees for customs.

Open an International eBay Store

f you're serious about international selling and have a target market in mind, it could make sense to open an international eBay store.

Let's say you are doing a booming business selling vintage concert t-shirts. Your two best international markets are Germany and the United Kingdom. You have just picked up a new line of custom-printed t-shirts, hoodies, bikinis, and other apparel items. The new items are selling well to buyers who like the vintage look but can't lay down several hundred dollars for a vintage t-shirt.

You know from experience that the majority of customers who buy your vintage look apparel discover it in your eBay store. Sales in the U. K. and Germany aren't taking off, but your marketing intern had a light bulb moment—What if you opened local eBay stores in those markets so you could cross-promote the vintage look apparel?

Bingo!

The best way to grow an international market is the same way you do it at home. Build an eBay store and cross-promote your items.

Set up a scrolling gallery at the bottom of every listing that features vintage-looking apparel. Mention the vintage look apparel in every listing, and invite customers to explore your eBay store for more great deals.

Set up listing headers that feature the new items. Build a storefront with clickable links to the new categories. Make it bold. Make it visual.

Use Markdown Manager to your advantage. Offer free shipping occasionally. Discount a different category every week or every month. Set up promotion boxes to highlight your specials.

If you set up an eBay store in a non-English-speaking country, find a translator to set up your listings and titles.

....

An eBay store is a slightly more expensive way to sell internationally, but the payoff could be immense if you can make a go of it.

The key to success is to localize the store to each market you sell in, cross-promote items as much as possible, and run frequent specials to build your brand.

Know Your Numbers

(*Much of this section was originally published in my book -
eBay Bookkeeping Made Easy. It's a primer on bookkeeping,
taxes, business types, and tax deductions. The information in
this section can save you thousands of dollars on your taxes
every year.*)

et Organized

GYou need a system to organize and store your
receipts and records. Some sellers use a file
cabinet. Some use expandable file folders. I like
to use loose-leaf binders. I get a five-inch
binder, monthly divider inserts, and storage pocket inserts.

Storing everything this way keeps all my business records
readily accessible, and the binder fits neatly on my bookshelf.
I can store fifteen years of business records side-by-side in a
relatively small space.

Save your receipts

Get used to it now. You need to save all your receipts.

When you buy something online, print out the invoice,
punch it with a three-hole punch, and store it in your three-
ring binder under the month of purchase.

Save all your mortgage or rent receipts, utility bills, phone bills, cable bills, sewer bills, etc. Store them in a zipper pouch in your binder. You're going to need them to file for the home office deduction. It will save you thousands of dollars on your taxes every year.

If you purchase supplies at Walmart, Staples, Office Depot, etc., save your receipts in a No. 10 envelope. Label the envelopes by month and store them in a zipper pouch in your binder.

Write down your mileage

Go to Walmart, Target, or your office supply superstore and buy a mileage log. They cost under five bucks and can save you close to a thousand dollars over the year.

Starting today – write down the beginning mileage on your vehicle. Every time you get in the car to run to the post office, pick up supplies, cruise a garage or estate sale, or anything related to your business – write it down. Record your beginning and ending mileage. Jot down a quick note about where you went or why you went there. It doesn't have to be a novel or anything fancy. Post Office, Bank, yard sale – just something to leave a trail of how it was business related.

Save all your auto-related receipts as well. The government lets you deduct your actual travel-related expenses or the mileage deduction (65.5¢ this year), whichever is greater. To ensure the largest deduction, you need to save your car payment stubs, insurance payment records, gas receipts, repair bills, oil change receipts, and anything related to your car. Grab another No. 10 envelope for each month, and label it auto expenses.

Claim your workspace

To claim the home office deduction, you need to devote a portion of your home exclusively to your online business. Pick a room, a portion of a room, your garage, basement, or whatever. Get everything not related to your business out of there, and set up your workspace.

Even if you create most of your listings sitting in the recliner in front of the TV, you need a separate room for storage, mailing, and quiet time. The space your chair occupies doesn't count as a work area for the home office deduction, and neither does the kitchen table if it doubles as a shipping center and a suppertime smorgasbord.

Open a business checking account.

You are running a business now. One of the first things you need to do is separate your business and financial expenses.

Open a business checking account. Get a business debit card and credit card. Having separate bank accounts does two things. In the case of an IRS audit, it shows them you are serious about your business. And two, it keeps you from nickel and diming your business to death. The minute you deposit your eBay money in your personal account, you're going to start spending it on a Starbucks coffee, a Mickey D's burger, whatever. If you want to track your business earnings and expenses accurately, you need to separate them from your personal money.

Separate Business & Personal Spending.

Don't make personal purchases with your business account—stop using it to buy pop, gas, groceries, etc. Use it for work-related tasks like when you pick up shipping supplies or purchase inventory for your business.

When you do slip up and make a personal purchase with your business account, make sure you label it as a personal expenditure. That way, it won't mess with your accounting records.

Set aside money to expand your business.

Once money starts pouring into your account, it's easy to get caught up in spending it. Decide upfront to reinvest a certain percentage of your profits into expanding your business, whether that means adding new product lines, upgrading your computer system, or updating your work area.

Do this today before the extra money becomes a part of your regular spending habits.

Make a plan, and work your plan

This one ties into setting money aside for business expansion.

After your business has been running for a while, it's time to sit down and develop a business plan. Decide where you want to be in six months, a year from now, and five years from now. It doesn't have to be a lengthy document. You can start by jotting down a few notes – I want to double my sales over the next eighteen months, or by this time next year, I want to be making $20,000 a year.

As time goes by, change and refine your plan. Make it more specific. Make a list of short-term and long-term targets, and check them off as you reach them.

In short, make a plan, and work your plan.

....

Bookkeeping should be an important part of your plan. Numbers measure business success.

You don't need to be an accounting genius to be successful selling online, but you do need to know enough to understand your numbers.

In the next section, I'm going to give you a list of accounting terms that can come in handy. The more you understand them, the better you will be at managing your business.

Here's the very least you need to know about accounting to run your business properly.

Accounting records get recorded in what's called a **general ledger**. It is a financial record of a company over a period. The information recorded in it is used by accountants and accounting programs to prepare financial statements.

Accountants use what's called a double-entry system. A debit on one side gets offset by a credit on the other side. The good news is with today's advanced software, business owners don't need to know anything about debits and credits. The program does all of the heavy lifting for you and crunches the numbers.

A **balance sheet** shows a company's assets, liabilities, and owner's equity at a given point in time. The simple formula behind the balance sheet is —

$$assets = liabilities + owner's\ equity$$

A **cash flow statement** shows all the money a company earns and spends over a period. Companies use cash flow projections to help manage their spending and ensure they have the required money on hand to cover their bills.

A profit and loss statement or **P & L statement** shows whether a business is profitable or not over a period. Companies prepare P & L statements monthly, quarterly, and yearly.

The general format for the P & L statement is to list income accounts at the top, then expenses, followed by a final line that shows the "bottom line" — or profit and loss.

If you understand these reports, you will be more in tune with the financial health of your business.

QuickBooks & FreshBooks

eBay has been all over the place with accounting solutions. They supported QuickBooks when I started selling, then ditched them for GoDaddy's accounting app. When GoDaddy shut down its accounting solution in 2022, eBay went back to working with QuickBooks.

QuickBooks is like the Swiss Army knife for eBay sellers when it comes to accounting. You can use it to track your sales, expenses, and inventory. Once you connect your eBay account to QuickBooks, it makes sharing data super easy.

After everything is linked up, you can organize and monitor your eBay sales within QuickBooks. This gives you a clear view of how much money is coming in and going out. Don't forget to log your fees and expenses so you get an accurate picture of your business's health.

QuickBooks sorts expenses to ensure your financial data shows where your money is going. You also should double-check everything by comparing your QuickBooks transactions to your actual bank statements.

If you want to keep a nice, neat financial history, you can attach receipts and docs to your transactions. And if you're dealing with sales tax stuff, QuickBooks can help calculate and track it, which is a lifesaver for tax time.

QuickBooks also comes with a bunch of financial reports like profit and loss statements and balance sheets. These are like treasure maps for your eBay business's finances.

Remember to enter your transactions regularly so QuickBooks stays up-to-date. And every now and then, make sure your QuickBooks and eBay accounts match up to catch any mistakes early.

Just by following these steps and using QuickBooks the right way, eBay sellers can keep their financial records straight, understand their business's money situation better, and make tax time and financial analysis a breeze.

Another advantage for QuickBooks users is that it integrates with TurboTax, transferring information to make tax time a breeze.

FreshBooks is another accounting solution used by many eBay sellers. It is your online money buddy for eBay. You set it up, connect your eBay store, and then, when you sell something, it tells FreshBooks about it, creating an online receipt.

FreshBooks is not just for sales, though – you can use it to keep track of all the costs of doing business, like what you spend on shipping and eBay fees. Plus, you can connect your bank account to help monitor where your money is going. FreshBooks sorts everything into categories, making it easy to track your sales and expenses.

The program provides a number of reports so you can see how you're doing financially. And when tax time rolls around, FreshBooks helps gather the info you need.

You can also check to make sure you get paid for everything you sell on eBay. And it gives you hints about whether you're making money or if there are areas you can improve.

FreshBooks isn't just about eBay, though– it's got other tricks, like time tracking and making invoices, that help you manage your money better. It's like a helpful friend for keeping your eBay finances in order! And it easily expands to track sales and expenses if you're selling off eBay.

Keep Records the Old-fashioned Way

What if you want to keep track of your income and expenses the old-fashioned way – using an Excel spreadsheet or a hand-written ledger?
No problem.

If you use Excel, you need to set up your income and expense categories the way accounting programs do. It should look something like this –

Income

- eBay sales

- Amazon Sales

- Etsy sales

- Bonanza sales

- bidStart sales

- Sales tax collected

- Shipping income

Expenses

- Cost of goods sold

- eBay fees

- Amazon fees

- Etsy fees

- Bonanza fees

- Internet expenses

- Phone

- Utilities

- Rent

- Computer equipment

- Software

- Professional fees

- Postage

- Mailing supplies

- Office supplies

Bottom Line

The easiest way to track your expenses is in a simple ledger style. Run your categories down the right-hand side of the page. Put your days across the top of the page. Leave room to subtotal your income and expenses. At the very bottom, you should have a space for your "bottom line" or profit and loss.

Assign a separate page for each month. At the end of each month, transfer all of the information over to a page with yearly totals. Excel users have an advantage here because you can set these items to update automatically.

What I have outlined here is a very simple system, but it will give you all the information you need to manage your business. By looking at your income and expenses, you should be able to spot trends and identify cash flow problems.

The best advice I can give you is to try to update your information every day or two. If you let it go until the end of the month, the task is going to seem overwhelming.

What You Need to Know About Taxes

Remember that old saying, "The only thing certain in life is death and taxes." Running a business is all about collecting and paying taxes.

Here are just a few of the different taxes you are going to be dealing with in your eBay business.

1) Sales & use taxes
2) Estimated taxes
3) Self-employment taxes
4) Unemployment tax
5) State and Federal Income Taxes

We are going to talk a little bit about each of these taxes – What they are? How they affect your business? And what you need to do to stay on the right side of the IRS and your local tax authorities.

1) **Sales & use taxes**. Forty-five states require residents to pay a sales tax when they purchase property within that state. If you are an online seller and make a sale within your home state, you are required by law to collect the proper sales tax

on it and remit the payment to your state tax authority. Failure to collect sales tax could put you on the wrong side of tax authorities if you get audited.

To collect taxes, you need to apply for a sales and use tax permit (sometimes called a resale permit) from your state. There is normally no charge for it, but some states may require you to make a deposit based on the volume of transactions you are expected to handle. It asks a few quick questions about your business, your sales channel, and your expected sales revenue. Once you receive your permit, you are required to collect tax on every transaction you process in your home state. Most states base your payment period upon your expected tax collections. As a result, you may have to remit payments monthly, quarterly, or annually.

For most sellers, this is no longer an issue. eBay now collects taxes for most sales that require it and remits the amount to the proper taxing authorities.

Use tax is one of the most misunderstood taxes. The way it's supposed to work is if you purchase something from outside of your home state and don't pay sales tax, you're supposed to fess up on your state income tax form and pay the appropriate tax. As you can probably guess, that rarely happens.

A good example of an item that would qualify for use tax is if you purchase your mailers from an out-of-state supplier on eBay. They ship them to you without charging sales tax. Because no sales tax was charged on this transaction when you purchased it, you are obligated to pay a use tax to make up for it.

The same thing is true for non-business owners. If you order clothes from a seller on eBay or Amazon and don't get charged sales tax, you are obligated to declare the transaction on your state income tax return and pay the appropriate sales tax on it.

If you intend to purchase items from a wholesaler, they will require you to provide them with a state tax ID. If you can't produce a tax ID, some wholesalers will refuse to do business with you, and others will insist on charging you sales tax on all of your purchases. You can also use your tax permit to eliminate sales taxes when you are purchasing items for resale from other retailers. So the next time you scoop up a cartload of closeouts at the outlet mall, you can save yourself a bundle by not having to pay the sales tax.

2) **Estimated taxes**. If you are self-employed, you are required to pay estimated taxes to the IRS and your state tax authority. Quarterly taxes are due April 15, July 15, October 15, and January 15. Tax programs such as TurboTax and HR Block will help you estimate your quarterly taxes. Most bookkeeping programs show you your estimated taxes due along with your sales tax liability.

Keep in mind most of these programs estimate your taxes based on last year's income or your trending income. If your income is sporadic or changes from year to year, you may want to consult with an accountant or tax advisor to ensure you're paying the proper amount.

If you pay less than a certain percentage of the amount that is due, you may wind up having to pay extra fees and penalties.

3) **Self-employment taxes** are similar to Social Security and Medicare taxes charged to people who work for an employer. The only difference is self-employed persons need to self-report these taxes and pay both the employer's and the employee's share.

Self-employment taxes get figured on Schedule SE of your IRS Form 1040. In 2014, the self-employment tax rate was 15.3% - 12.4% for Social Security and 2.9% for Medicare. In 2023, the amount of income subject to the portion of Social Security tax was capped at $160,200. There is no cap for the Medicare tax portion of self-employment tax.

You can deduct the employer portion of your self-employment tax (approximately 50 percent) when you figure your adjusted gross income for Federal taxes.

4) **Unemployment taxes**. If you hire employees to work in your online business, you are required to pay unemployment taxes. These vary by state. Just keep in mind there is a separate state and Federal tax due.

See Publication 926 for more information and a list of state taxing authorities.
http://www.irs.gov/publications/p926/index.html

5) **Federal and state taxes**. When most online sellers think about taxes, these are what come to mind.

Some online sellers try to avoid paying income taxes on their earnings or think taxes are just for big-time sellers. The truth is if you make as little as one dollar selling online, you are required to report it for income tax purposes.

To keep everyone honest, the government imposed mandatory reporting requirements upon PayPal, eBay, Amazon, and other online platforms. If more than $600 gets deposited into your account during the year, the merchant is required to report it to the IRS on Form 1099-K.

....

That's the very least you need to know about taxes and your online business. Here are a few more tips that can help you out when the time comes to prepare your Federal and state tax forms.

Business income gets reported on Schedule C of your Form 1040.

Several tax programs are available to make filing your business taxes easier. The two I've had the most experience working with are TurboTax Business and H R Block Premium or H R Block Premium & Business. Each of these programs will conduct a fact-finding interview with you about your business and walk you step-by-step through filing your tax return.

Even if you use an accountant or tax preparer, doing your taxes first can save you hundreds of dollars when it comes time to file. This way, all of the information is gathered together and entered in the correct areas on your tax return. All your tax professional needs to do is review everything to ensure there is nothing you overlooked or left out.

Most Common Tax Deductions

One of the perks of being a business owner is the ability to shift some of your income by taking advantage of various business deductions. Here are some of the most common business deductions taken by online business owners.

Home Office Deduction. Many business owners are afraid to claim the home office deduction because they have heard the IRS targets filers who take it. That's pretty much one of those urban legends that get bigger every time it's told.

The home office deduction is every online seller's best friend and can save you thousands of dollars on your taxes if you use it properly.

Here are the IRS rules for taking the home office deduction:

1) Your home must be your principal place of business.
2) You must use the area of your home (a room or portion of a room) exclusively to conduct business. If you do all your work at your kitchen table, you don't qualify for the home office deduction because you don't use that area exclusively for business. If, on the other hand, you devote an extra bedroom, basement, or garage exclusively to conducting the activities of

your online business—this space would qualify for the home office deduction.

To learn more about the home office deduction, you can check out Publication 587.
http://www.irs.gov/publications/p587/index.html
The methods for calculating the home office deduction change frequently, so even if you have taken it in the past, you may want to brush up on the new guidelines.

Mileage Deduction. If you use your vehicle while conducting your business, you can deduct your expenses. Business owners can take either the standard mileage deduction or deduct the actual expenses incurred for the use of the vehicle in their business.

To take the mileage deduction, you need to record all the miles your car is driven for personal and business use. I would recommend purchasing a mileage log. You can find one in the office supply section at Walmart or Target or at larger office supply stores such as Office Max, Staples, or Office Depot. They run about $5.00 and are small enough to slip under your visor or into your glove box.

Each time you head to the post office, run to the store for mailing supplies, or to a yard sale or estate sale to pick up new inventory, make sure to record your beginning and ending mileage.

In 2023, the standard mileage deduction was 65.5¢ per business mile driven, up from 62.5¢ in 2022. If you opt to deduct actual expenses, make sure to record all of your expenses for car payments, insurance, repairs, tires, oil changes, and gasoline. You can then deduct the percentage of expenses based on the miles driven for business usage.

Travel. Did you ever want to visit California or Hawaii but weren't sure you could afford it?. The cost of travel is fully deductible if it is business-related.

Let's say you are ready for a vacation, and eBay is throwing a seller get-together in Scottsdale. You can deduct all your expenses – airfare, car rentals, cabs, motels, food, and admission – as long as they are related to the event. If your spouse helps out in your business, their expenses are covered as well. If you decide to make a real vacation of it and bring the kids along, too, you would not be able to deduct expenses for their travel, food, lodging, etc., if they do not participate in the business.

The travel expense deduction can also be used to cover day trips out of town. If you visit an estate sale or auction several hundred miles away, all your expenses related to the buying trip would be deductible. Again, if you bring along the kids or someone unrelated to your business, their expenses will not be covered.

Computers, printers, office supplies. Are you a techie? Have you always wanted to own the latest, greatest gadgets but wished you had a rich uncle to help you out with the payments?

Uncle Sam can come to the rescue here, too. You can deduct the price of a new computer, printer, cell phone, iPad, or any other gadget that you regularly use in your online business. The only hitch is the item needs to be for your business use only.

You have the option of depreciating the expense of your purchase over the expected life of the item, or in most cases, you can deduct the full value of the item.

Internet, cell phone, etc. If you purchase a separate cell phone or internet service for your business, you can deduct the full cost as a business expense. If you use them for business and personal use, you can only deduct the portion of the service you use for business.

If you're on track to make a little too much money this year and are worried about paying extra taxes, look at some of these ideas as ways to shift your tax burden. Once again, don't go crazy. Before you rush off on that junket to Hawaii or Europe, consult with your tax advisor first to ensure the trip is deductible in your situation.

....

Here are two other suggestions while we're talking about tax deductions. You can use your business income to help fund your retirement or to shift money to your kids by employing them to work in your business.

When you own your own business, you can fund a personal retirement account, 401K, SEP IRA, or KEOGH. The individual details are beyond the scope of this book; consult a tax professional for more details.

If you have kids, put them to work for your company and pay them the money you would have given them anyway. If you have college-age kids, this is a good way to help them pay their way through college while deducting the expenses from your business. Keep in mind when you do this, it is just like hiring a regular employee. You need to pay unemployment taxes and provide a W-2 at the end of the year.

Business Permits, Licenses, and Such

Most eBay sellers run their businesses out of their homes. Their neighbors don't know anything about it except for the frequent comings and goings of the mail trucks, UPS vans, and Fed Ex guys.

As such, most eBay sellers don't bother with licenses or permits. They go about their daily routine pretty much unaware they may be breaking local codes and regulations.

What I'm going to do here is talk a little bit about the different licenses and permits a typical eBay business owner might bump up against and give you a few tips on how to get them.

DBA (Doing Business As). If you conduct your business using an assumed (fictitious) name, you are required to record your information with the city clerk's office or county clerk's office, depending on where you live. Sometimes, you can fill out the form online. Other times, you will be required to go to the appropriate office and pay a small fee. They check to see if the name is in use by another company. If it is, you need to pick a new name. Banks will require a copy of your DBA if you attempt to open an account in your business's name.

Business License. Most cities and counties require a license to conduct business within their boundaries. The fees vary based on the type of business you run. Where I live, you apply for a license with the city's Department of Revenue. If you are unsure where to apply for a business license in your area, Google "city name business license."

EIN (Employer Identification Number). Most online businesses conduct their business using the owner's social security number. If you prefer not to share that information, you can apply to the IRS for an EIN. Here is a link to apply for an EIN online: https://www.us-tax-id-number.com/?gclid=CJaB3Kq_jr4CFckWMgod63cAbQ.

Home Business Permit. Some municipalities require homeowners to register if they are conducting business out of their homes. Call your city clerk's office to learn more about your area's licensing requirements.

Sales & Use Tax Permit. If you make sales to residents within the boundaries of your state, you will be required to collect sales tax. Contact your state Department of Revenue for more information.

Again, eBay collects sales tax in most localities now, so most sellers don't need to worry about them.

Choose Your Business Structure

How you structure your business plays a key role in how much money you will keep at the end of the year.

Most eBay businesses will take one of the following structures.

1) Sole proprietorship
2) Partnership
3) Corporation
4) Small business corporation (Subchapter S)

Sole proprietorship

A sole proprietorship is the simplest form of business entity. One person runs it with no distinction between the individual and the business. If the business makes money, you keep all of the profits. If the business loses money, you are responsible for all of the losses.

Most sole proprietorships are conducted using the business owner's name. If you choose to run it under a different name, you may need to file a DBA (Doing Business As). Normally, you would register your business with the City Clerk's Office or a county office and pay a small fee. They will check to see if the name you want to use is already in use. If another business is using it, you will need to choose another name.

Your business income should be recorded on Schedule C of your IRS 1040 tax form and would get taxed at your normal rate.

The major disadvantage of a sole proprietorship is you are 100% responsible for business liabilities. If you sell defective products or someone gets hurt on your business premises, you are fully responsible and could get sued for liability.

Partnership

A partnership is a business relationship between two or more people. Partners normally sign a partnership agreement. Each of them contributes a certain amount of capital and labor and shares in the profits or losses of the business.

Partners can share equally in the profits, or certain partners may have a larger percentage of ownership based on the partnership agreement. Income gets reported to each partner on a form called a Schedule K-1.

The disadvantage is partners are fully responsible for any liabilities contracted by the business.

Corporation

A corporation is an independent legal entity owned by its shareholders. The business gets registered with the State Corporation Department or Secretary of State's Office. They are required to have business licenses and permits and to file quarterly and annual reports with the state they are incorporated in.

Corporations are normally owned by a large number of people who have issued shares in exchange for investing capital in the business.

Shareholders in the corporation receive income in the form of dividends. The biggest advantage of a corporation is income gets taxed at a lower corporate rate, and liability is limited to the money you have invested in the corporation.

Subchapter S Corporation

Subchapter S corporations pass earnings and losses through to shareholders for federal tax purposes. Shareholders report income on their personal tax returns and pay taxes at their normal rate.

To qualify as an S Corporation, the corporation must file Form 2553 Election by a Small Business Corporation. http://www.irs.gov/pub/irs-pdf/f2553.pdf

S Corporations have many advantages that make them attractive to online business owners.

1) Your assets are protected. The most you can lose as an investor is the money you have invested in the corporation.
2) Ability to reduce self-employment tax liability by paying yourself a portion of income as salary and as dividends.
3) Pass through taxation, which allows owners to report losses or earnings on their personal tax returns.

4) It opens new possibilities in offering yourself corporate perks such as better retirement plans, writing off college expenses, and other benefits. Be sure to consult with a qualified tax advisor before implementing any of these ideas.

Most online businesses begin life as a sole proprietorship and scale up as the business grows.

Bonus Article: Sell it on Amazon

The best thing about Amazon is the low cost of entry. Unlike eBay and many other online commerce sites, Amazon doesn't have separate listing fees for the items you put up for sale. As a result, sellers can add thousands of items to their Amazon store without paying fees until they sell something.

Another great thing about selling on Amazon is you can list most of your items in one minute or less. You don't have to snap any pictures. You don't have to write a detailed item description. Selling your item on Amazon is as simple as hitching a ride on the Amazon listing page.

It's easy to spot the items listed by individual sellers. When you see a box like the one below, the items sold by Amazon are listed under Amazon's price. The items offered by individual sellers are in the following two categories.

Formats	Amazon price	New from	Used from
Kindle Edition	$3.77	--	--
Paperback	$10.54 *Prime*	$10.54	$14.39

What I want to do first is take a minute to walk you through listing a typical item for sale on Amazon. Then, I will give you some pointers about maximizing your sales there.

Listing your first item on Amazon

Type the name or the description of the item you want to sell into the Amazon search bar. Click on the thing you want to sell. Off to the right-hand side, you will see a small box labeled **More Buying Choices**. At the bottom of this box, click on the **Sell on Amazon** button.

```
        More Buying Choices
      9 used & new from $10.54
   Have one to sell?  Sell on Amazon
```

At this point, you're eight steps away from listing your item for sale on Amazon.

Step 1. Amazon shows you the title and picture of the item you selected and asks you to verify this is the correct item you want to sell. You don't need to do anything if it's the right item.

Step 2. Tell customers your item's condition. Click on the radio button in the box labeled **condition** and select the one that best describes the condition of your item.

Below this, you have a chance to add a comment about the condition of your item. For example, suppose you are selling a textbook. In that case, you could say, "Overall, excellent condition, but it does have some highlighting in the first three chapters."

Step 3. Amazon shows you the lowest price the item is being sold for and the lowest shipping price available for it. In most cases, you will find that Amazon has the lowest price, especially if you sell new items and offer free shipping (with Amazon Prime). Don't panic! Many people will still buy from you, even if your price is higher and you charge shipping.

Step 4. Enter your selling price. Next to the box where you enter your selling price, Amazon shows how much they will charge your customer for shipping.

Step 5. Tell Amazon how many items you have for sale.

Step 6. This step tells Amazon to collect taxes if you have enabled them to do so. Casual sellers can skip this step. Instead, Amazon collects taxes in the states that require it.

Step 7. Enter your SKU (stock-keeping unit). This is how you identify the item you are listing for sale. I have over 10,000 items available for sale on Amazon. All of them are numbered and stored on storage shelves. I can go to that shelf whenever one sells and quickly pull the item for shipping.

When you are just starting an SKU isn't all that important, but if you intend to grow your business, you should start thinking about using some type of labeling system.

Amazon assigns one for you if you decide not to enter an SKU.

Step 8. Select your shipping methods. Amazon requires you to add a basic shipping service. Adding additional shipping options can help you sell more items. I suggest choosing Expedited Shipping (priority mail) and the first international shipping option (first class).

At this point, you're almost done. Press the yellow **Continue** button at the bottom.

This takes you to a screen to review your selling information. The last few boxes show you Amazon's commission when your item sells, how much Amazon allows you for shipping, and how much money you will receive (including your shipping credit) after Amazon's commission is taken out.

If everything looks good, press the **Submit your listing** button.

The next thing you're going to see is **Congratulations! You've successfully listed _____.**

That's it. Your item is now listed for sale on Amazon.

You can sit back and wait for the sales to start rolling in, or better yet, list more items so you can make more sales.

For most items you sell, that is all there is to sell on Amazon.

How to add an item to the Amazon catalog

Suppose you sell unique items that aren't already in the Amazon catalog. In that case, Amazon lets you add an item description page to their catalog. While it's not hard to do, it does take a little extra time and effort, so I will cover this in more detail.

To add an item to the Amazon catalog, you need to visit Seller Central and place your mouse over **Inventory**. Then, at the drop-down menu, select **Add a Product**.

This allows you to search the Amazon catalog to see if it is already listed. Suppose your item is not currently available on Amazon. In that case, you can add a new item by clicking on **Create a new product**.

Select a category to list your item in. You can search for a category or browse through a list of categories. Choose the category that most closely fits your item.

After selecting the category you want to list your item in, you will be taken to the Sell Your Item dashboard.

* Vital Info	* Offer	Images	Description	Keywords	More Details

All Product Categories > Everything Else > Other Products > Other Products   [Next]

* Product Name: [_____]
(Max. 250 characters. Please include the size and color of the item in the   Example: Tommy Bahama 'Shades of Paradise' Polo Large Blue
Product Name, if available.)

Manufacturer: [_____]
  Example: Sony, Kitchen Aid, Microsoft

Brand Name: [_____]
(Max. 50 characters)   Example: Ralph Lauren, North Face, Patagonia

Model Number: [_____]
(Product code assigned by the manufacturer; can be numbers, letters, or both)   Example: C-50

Manufacturer Part Number: [_____]
(For most products, this will be identical to the model number; however, some   Example: LE
manufacturers distinguish part number from model number.)

Package Quantity: [_____]
(Quantity of the item for sale in one package)   Example: 2

UPC or EAN: [_____]

  [Next]

[Cancel] [Save and finish]

Provide as much information as possible under each of the six tabs at the top of your dashboard. Try to fill in every box you can because Amazon will use your information to show your item in relevant search requests.

At the very least, you need to fill in the boxes with a red star to the left of them.

Vital Info. What you put here is going to become the title for your listing. Make sure it is keyword-rich and describes your item correctly. You have 250 characters to state your case. Make the most of it. Give the name, manufacturer, model number, color, accessories, and other familiar names your item might be known by.

The manufacturer is exactly what it says. If you know who made your item, list it here. If you know the brand name, enter it in the following line. Next, enter the model number and manufacturer number if they are available. Package quantity means how many are packaged together – one, two, or a dozen. Finally, the UPC or EAN is the manufacturer's product code. If you know the UPC code, enter it here.

Offer. List your selling price—just below that, you can offer a sale price for a limited period. Enter the sale price, and select the days you would like the sale to run. Enter how many items you have. If you have a sales tax permit, enter the pertinent info so that Amazon can collect sales tax from your buyers.

Handling time means how many days it will be before shipping the item. Amazon's default is one or two days, so list it here if it takes longer to get your item ready to ship. An example of this would be if you use a drop shipper, and it takes some time for the order to process through their system.

The selling date is when you want the item listed on Amazon. Gift options: Will you gift wrap the item or include a card with it. Select the services you wish to offer. Restock date means if you are out of stock when will more be available.

Import designations tell buyers where your item was made. Several choices are available. Read through them and choose the most appropriate one for what you are selling.

Next, you need to choose your shipping method. You can ship the item or offer fulfillment by Amazon (FBA). FBA means you ship your products to Amazon when you list them, and Amazon handles shipping and fulfillment for you. The biggest advantage is that your items often qualify for Amazon's free shipping offers, including Amazon Prime. Another advantage is many buyers are more comfortable buying from you because your item ships to them directly from Amazon.

I will talk about Fulfillment by Amazon and how it can help to increase your sales in more detail later in this chapter.

Images. You need to include at least one photo of your item. The more pictures you include, the better your chances of selling your item. Picture requirements are listed next to the uploading tool.

When getting pictures ready to upload, you should keep in mind the following:

- Only show the exact item you are selling. Do not include any extra items or props in your pictures.
- Watermarks are not allowed.
- You cannot superimpose any text over your images.
- Your main image must be a photo. Drawings are not allowed.
- All pictures should be a minimum of 1000 x 500 pixels. Buyers cannot zoom in on smaller images, so they will not have close-up views of what you are selling.
- J-Peg illustrations are the preferred file type.

Description. The description section is broken down into two sections. One is for product features, and the next section is for your actual written description of the item.

Features give more information about your item and are listed in bullet points on the item description page. Here are some of the features provided for the Apple iPad to give you an idea of what type of features you should list with your items:

- Apple's newest generation of iPads
- 9.7-inch (diagonal) LED glossy back-lit screen
- Forward-facing and rear-camera
- Apple IOS 4 and access to the Apple Apps Store
- 1 GHz dual-core Apple A5 custom-designed processor

Your description should be written in a narrative style and product-focused. You are not allowed to include any information about your business.

Once you list your item, the item description page becomes part of the Amazon catalog. Therefore, any seller with the same item can list it alongside yours on the same item description page.

Keywords. Keywords are similar to tags you put on your items to help buyers find them in search. You can skip the first section of keywords as it is only available to Platinum Sellers.

Search terms are the keywords buyers will use to search for your items. Include all obvious ones: Product name, model #, manufacturer, color, and size. If you have trouble thinking of keywords, visit the Google Keyword Tool. It will help you pick keywords people use to search for your item.

Another word of advice—don't use single-word search terms. Instead, use "long-tail keywords" whenever possible. Long-tail keywords are more specific and encompass most of the searches made on Google. Some examples of long-tail keywords are: "Space exploration in the Milky Way Galaxy,"

"How to write better keywords," and "How to make money on Kindle."

The following section helps Amazon determine how your product is used and on what occasions it is used. This allows Amazon to show your items in a variety of searches.

More Details. This section lets you add more product-specific information. Some categories include Brand, MSRP, Part number, model number, and is your item subject to prop. 65 reporting in California, shipping weight, product and shipping size specifications, and the like. Specific information is based on the type of product you are selling.

When you are done, press **Save and finish**. Your item is now listed for sale on Amazon.

It sounds complicated, but it will be a lot easier after you've added two or three products to the catalog.

The biggest problem when I add custom pages is that there's no real-time preview like you have on eBay. It can take a half-hour or more for the listing page to display on Amazon, so you have to check back later to ensure everything posted okay. Another problem is that pictures can take ten or fifteen minutes to upload, so you're stuck waiting before you can work on your next product listing.

That pretty much covers listing your items on Amazon.

If you have a large catalog of items, you can upload them through a spreadsheet. In addition, several services help eBay sellers move their entire eBay store to Amazon.

One such service I have had experience with is Export Your Store.

I like using Export Your Store because they do all the heavy lifting for you. The bad thing about using Export Your Store is that Amazon is nothing like eBay, so after they transfer your items to Amazon, you still have a lot of work to ensure everything is properly optimized.

Here are a few differences between eBay and Amazon that can cause problems.

- Amazon is a marketplace. Therefore, they don't allow personal branding or HTML code on item description pages.
- Amazon doesn't allow references to your business in their item description pages.
- Amazon requires tags (keywords) to be entered in the proper section of their listing form to help buyers find your item in a search.

The folks at Export Your Store are really good at stripping the HTML code out of your listings and getting them moved over to eBay. I had over ten thousand items exported from eBay to Amazon in just over two days.

Then, I started receiving a stream of item violation warnings from Amazon. When I did this, you could still have your customer service email address in your eBay listings. This violated Amazon's terms of service, and I was forced to go through just over 10,000 items, one at a time, and edit each of them individually.

Three weeks of hell followed, spending twelve to fourteen hours daily checking, revising, and deleting listings.

Another problem was that when they stripped the HTML code from my listing templates, they removed part of my item descriptions, including the SKU numbers. As a result, I had to add keywords to every Amazon listing. I think this was because I sell one-of-a-kind collectibles, and each item required adding a new page to the Amazon catalog. Of course, this would not be an issue if you sell more traditional items, like electronics, books, CDs, or DVDs that already have a catalog page.

I would still recommend Export Your Store with all the problems I mentioned. Customer service was responsive and worked quickly to help solve any issues.

Several other companies can help you export your eBay store items to Amazon. Two of them are Vendio and Linnworks.

Amazon FBA

Amazon FBA (Fulfillment by Amazon) can help skyrocket your sales. According to a study conducted by Amazon, 64% of people who have used Fulfillment by Amazon have increased their sales by 20% or more.

When you use Fulfillment by Amazon, Amazon becomes customer service central for your business.

Here are the top benefits you receive by using FBA:

1. Your items become eligible for FREE Super Saver Shipping and Amazon Prime Benefits

2. Your FBA items are displayed with no shipping charges, giving you the benefit of being a lower-priced seller.
3. Your back end is taken care of by Amazon. They handle all of the shipping, returns, and customer service problems for you.
4. Your items become eligible to compete for the Buy Box.

Using FBA frees up more time to source new products and enjoy life more.

You ship your inventory to Amazon's warehouse. Once they receive your items in their inventory, they go for sale on Amazon. Each time one of your items sells, you will see it show up in your seller dashboard, but the good folks at Amazon do all of the work for you. They collect your payment. They ship the order for you and handle all customer service issues or returns.

Compare that with being an eBay Top Rated Seller who must ship their item with a one-day handling time to receive their 20% final discount fee. eBay sellers are chained to their computers, while Amazon FBA sellers are free to enjoy life without the constant rush to ship and handle customer service issues.

FBA is also a great deal for Amazon buyers.

FBA assures customers they will receive a great experience when buying from you. Most of the items sold through FBA are eligible for Amazon Super Saver Shipping and other Amazon Prime Benefits, including free shipping on orders over $25.00.

How to get started with FBA

To get started using FBA:

1. List your items in Seller Central, and select Fulfillment by Amazon as your shipping choice.
2. If you already have the item for sale on Amazon, go to **Manage Your Inventory** on your Seller Central Dashboard. Then, select the product that you want to include as FBA.
3. Print the labels provided by Amazon to ship your items to their warehouse.
4. When Amazon receives and scans your items into its inventory, they go live and are ready for sale.

Bonus Article: Sell it on Fiverr

Fiverr is a freelance marketplace where buyers and sellers can exchange cash for services. What amazes me is every item featured on Fiverr is $5.00—almost. There appears to be no limit to the types of services sellers can offer on Fiverr. Among the recent gigs (what Fiverr calls listings) are –

- Custom logo design
- Facebook header design
- Amazon book reviews and product reviews
- Puppet videos
- Kindle and eBook book covers
- Tarot readings
- Psychic readings
- Resume and cover letter writing
- Poetry Writing
- Business card design
- Infographic design

By now, hopefully, you get the idea. If you can imagine it, you can find a way to offer it as a gig on Fiverr.

The very least you need to know

Fiverr is relatively new to the e-commerce scene.

Micha Kaufman and Shai Wininger founded the company in 2010. Every gig starts at $5.00, but that's changing as the site continues to reinvent itself. Sellers receive $4.00 for each completed gig. Fiverr's take is twenty percent or $1.00 from each five-dollar gig.

As of October 2016, there were over three million gigs listed on Fiverr.

Fiverr has a leveling system, like eBay's Top-Rated Seller Program.

- **Newbies** have limited options on Fiverr. They can offer two gig extras limited to $5.00, $10.00, and $20.00. New sellers are limited to accepting four gigs in one transaction.

- **Level One** status opens up more opportunities for sellers. To reach Level One status, sellers need to complete ten gigs in the previous thirty days with a minimum 90% satisfaction rating. After they level up, sellers can list up to 15 gigs at a time, offer "fast delivery" for extra profits, and provide custom orders up to $1500. Level One status also opens up another gig extra—for a total of three and allows sellers to accept eight orders in one transaction.

- **Level Two Sellers** are required to have completed 50 gigs in the last sixty days with a minimum 90% satisfaction rating. When they reach this level, sellers have the chance to increase their income significantly. Buyers can purchase up to twelve of their gigs at one time. Gig Extras jump to five, and the price range jumps to $5.00, $10.00, $20.00, and $40,00.

- Becoming a **Top-Rated Seller** is like receiving tenure at a major university. The process for reaching this status is somewhat mysterious. The Fiverr blog states the site editors "mutually" choose Top Rated Sellers. What is clear, though, is once you receive this designation, a whole new world of profit possibilities opens up to you. Top-rated sellers can charge up to $100 for each gig extra, and they receive the Top-Rated Seller Badge next to each of their gigs.

If you are serious about making money on Fiverr, you need to level up as quickly as possible. The easiest way to do this is to offer a large selection of gigs and provide excellent customer service.

Gig Extras

Earlier, I mentioned gig extras.

Gig extras are the method Fiverr has devised to let sellers take their income to the next level. To better understand how gig extras work, check out these extras offered by Professor Puppet.

Get more with my Gig Extras

☐ I will post your video on YouTube so you don't have to OR   +$10
Deliver your video in 1080p HD PLEASE SPECIFY
Requires no additional time

☐ I will superimpose your URL or any message over your video   +$10
Limit 2 supers per upgrade
Requires no additional time

☐ I will Shoot your video on my Green Screen and superimpose a   +$50
different background
Requires no additional time

☐ I will RUSH SERVICE, I will drop everything and make your   +$20
video FIRST before anything else in the queue
Requires no additional time

Even though every gig starts at $5.00, Professor Puppet can increase his take to $95.00 if someone adds all his gig extras to their order.

And, just in case you think most buyers stick with the basic $5.00 offer, think again! Professor Puppet has made two promotional videos for my business. Each time, I spent over $35.00.

So, if anyone out there is still wondering how you can make money selling each of your services for only five bucks, you know the answer – **GIG EXTRAS**. They can easily raise your average $5.00 sale to $25.00 or more.

One final thought on gig extras. The best gig extras don't necessarily have to cost you more time or money.

Most sellers offer very simple gig extras:

- Next-day service for five or ten dollars
- A PSD file of the graphic they already designed for an extra $5.00 to $20.00. It's no extra work – you already have it on your computer.

- Two extra revisions for $5.00 or $10.00.
- Your video is delivered in additional formats for $10.00 or $20.00.
- A 3D cover to go with the 2D eBook cover they already designed for an additional $5.00.

The key to making the most money on Fiverr is to keep your gig extras simple and easy to perform but still make them appear valuable to your customers.

I saved the best part for last. Many sellers dangle a new-fangled cyber tip jar out there that lets them collect even more money.

Do you want to make even more money? The key is to give customers a compelling or downright crazy reason to give you an extra-large tip.

One seller suggests an extra $5.00 would let him start his day with a latte from Starbucks. For $20.00, he could put half a tank of gas in his old jalopy, and for $50.00, he would have a good start at taking his wife out for a romantic supper.

Who could resist giving this creative genius a tip?

Getting Started

Getting started as a seller on Fiverr is as easy as entering your email address and choosing a username and password. That's it, and you're a member of the Fiverr community.

Before you click the join button, take a few moments to think about your username. It is how people will come to know you on Fiverr.

A relevant username that complements the service you are providing will help position you as an expert in the service you are offering.

Many people choose the first idea that pops into their head or maybe their name. The thing is, if you name your business marysue or wonderwoman 113, people aren't going to have any idea what you do.

If you call yourself videoreviewer or bestlogodesigner, people are going to know right away what services you offer. A professional username can help position you as the right seller.

Seller Basics

Every gig on Fiverr starts with the words "I will ____for ____."

As a seller, your job is to fill in the blanks. Just what is it you're willing to do for five bucks? Ten bucks? Twenty bucks? Or whatever?

I know, some of you are saying – not much.

A recent Fiverr survey says there are thousands of sellers making $1000 to $2000, or more, every month selling their services on Fiverr. Some of the elite sellers make $5000 or more each and every month.

So, before you turn your nose up at five bucks, let's examine some of the things you need to consider before creating your first gig.

Before you do anything, check the Fiverr website for two or three days. Explore categories, and click into as many gigs as you can.

Keep your pen and notebook handy. Whenever you see something you like or something you think you might want to do – jot it down.

Write down the seller's username – the title of their gig – keywords they use to describe their gig – and any special instructions they include in their descriptions. It's information you can use to craft your gigs.

Don't stop there. Check out the pictures or samples they include. If the seller has a video describing the service they are offering, watch it and make a few notes about what they say and how they describe their gig.

Study the feedback left for gigs like yours. What did buyers like or dislike about them? Look for clues to help you design a better gig and position yours so more people will choose to do business with you.

You don't have to pick out your first gig right now. Just get down as many ideas as you can.

Look over the gigs you examined.

Draw a star by the ones you think would be a good fit for you. Cross off the ones you don't think would be a good fit for you or you can't see yourself doing.

This is where the rubber meets the road. At this point, you should have at least five gigs you think would give you a great start on Fiverr.

Make sure the gigs you choose are something you can make money doing.

Most sellers agree to make money, you need to offer a service you can complete in no more than fifteen minutes. Five minutes or less is even better.

At fifteen minutes per gig and an average profit of $4.00 per gig, that means you can make $16.00 per hour. If you can lower your working time to ten minutes per gig, you can make $24.00 per hour.

Now, go back and evaluate the gig ideas you picked out. Be brutally honest.

Is this something you can do in fifteen minutes or less? If not, is there a way you can do it faster? If not, scratch this gig off your list or move it to your work on later pile.

Continue to evaluate each potential gig the same way.

If you're sure you can complete them in fifteen minutes or less, great! Add them to your list of must-do gigs.

The last step is to work on a couple of your potential gigs to make sure how fast you can do them. Use a stopwatch to track your time. Make a list of your gigs by how much time they took you to complete.

Pick the gig you want to get started on today.

From here on out, we are going to concentrate on getting this gig ready to post on Fiverr.

Create Your First Gig

Posting a gig on Fiverr consists of nine simple steps.

For this demonstration, we're going to assume you're going to sell a Kindle book cover. As we walk through the steps, take some time to reflect on each step and how the process relates to creating your gig.

The gig shown below is from one of my favorite cover designers. Right now, she has 86 covers waiting in her queue over the next three days, so you know this lady is breaking her ass to get them done, but at the same time, she's making some serious bucks.

To get started, choose the Start Selling button at the top of Fiverr's main page.

Step 1. The first thing you're going to see is the familiar words, "I will _____ for $5.00."

Tell people what you're willing to do for $5.00. A good gig title should be short, tell people exactly what you are going to do for them, and be rich in keywords.

Look at the title for this gig. "I will design a professional and unique eBook cover or Kindle cover for $5.00."

It's a great title. It contains three main keywords: "design," "eBook cover," and "Kindle cover." It also has two descriptors or adjectives: "professional" and "unique."

The right keywords will give it a great shot at being picked up and shown by Fiverr's search engine every time someone searches for either "eBook cover" or "Kindle cover."

Step 2. Select a category. The beautiful thing here is Fiverr makes selecting a category super-easy. They only give you twelve choices: Fun and bizarre, Online Marketing, Graphics and Design, Advertising, Writing and translation, Lifestyle, Business, Programming and tech, Other, Music and audio, Gifts, and Video and Animation.

Choose the category that will give you the best bang for your buck.

Step 3. Description. Tell your story. Tell people what you are selling, what the benefits are for them, and what information you need from them to make it happen. If there are things you cannot or will not do, this is the place to say it. A lot of sellers that offer art and writing services specify they won't write or draw pornography. Remember, it's your business, and what you choose to do or not do is up to you.

Let's look at the description in our sample listing.

"Over 5,000 covers created to date! 3D Covers are FREE, and when I say three days, I mean three days – regardless of the orders in the queue…and I'm not happy until you are so

UNLIMITED REVISIONS! Order now! * I also create covers for ALL genres, so let's hear what you have in mind. What makes my covers stand out from other designers here on Fiverr? I treat your cover as an individual! Are cars the theme of your book? How do metallic fonts and backgrounds sound? Chocolate the theme? We'll make book buyers want to lick the cover itself! Trust me; you'll love your cover. Order now!"

What do you think?

This description offers so many examples of the things you should try to include in each and every one of your gig descriptions. The seller tells you twice to "Order Now!" She tells you once in the middle of the description and again at the end.

She emphasizes her covers are different from those made by other designers on Fiverr. Then she tells you what makes them better and different – "We'll make book buyers want to lick the cover itself!"

She guarantees buyers will be pleased with their cover. "I'm not happy until you are so UNLIMITED REVISIONS!"

Take some time to read through the descriptions written by many different Top-Rated Sellers, and you will quickly learn the secrets to being more successful and selling more gigs on Fiverr.

Step 4. Instructions to Buyer. Tell buyers what information you need to put their gig together.

Fiverr uses this box to request information from buyers, so before you fill it out, take a few minutes to carefully decide what information you need to make the buyer's project come together. The clearer you are with your instructions, the easier it will be to complete your project in as little time as possible.

Another benefit will be better feedback because you completed your gig on time and how the buyer wanted it.

Step 5. Tags. Tags are simply a list of keywords people use to search for your gig on Fiverr.

The easiest way to pick your tags is to see what keywords other sellers are using to tag their gigs. Choose the keywords you think are relevant and add them here.

Step 6. Maximum days to complete. What's the longest it will take you to deliver the finished gig? As a new seller, you should strive to deliver every gig within twenty-four hours.

People like fast. Everybody wants to buy something today and get it yesterday. Many buyers will choose your gig over someone else's when you offer one-day service, especially when other sellers list a three to five-day turnaround.

Only offer a one-day turnaround if you can deliver on it. You will hurt your rankings and increase your chances of receiving negative feedback if you deliver late. If you're not sure you can deliver your gig in one day, decide how many days you think it will take you to complete your gig, and then shoot to deliver as soon as you can. That will give buyers a pleasant surprise, and happy buyers mean good reviews.

Step 7. Add image. Upload images to illustrate your gig. These should be the best samples of your work. For illustrations, Fiverr recommends a .jpeg format, 600 pixels wide x 370 pixels high, with a maximum file size of 5 megabytes. Once you have your pictures ready, you can use MS Paint or another graphics program to resize them to 600 x 370 pixels.

It is also recommended you upload a video. It can be something as simple as talking about how you produce your gigs, giving instructions on the information you need from the seller to bring their gig to life, or a collage showing your gigs and comments from the people who purchased them.

Keep it simple. Be informative. Better yet, make it humorous.

Step 8. This item requires shipping. If you are sending a physical product to buyers, such as a small craft, check this box.

Step 9. Press the **Save** button.

Before you decide to press save, take a few minutes to look it over first.

- Did you spell everything correctly?
- Did you include enough keywords in your title and description?
- Are your tags or keywords ones that buyers will use to search for your gig?
- Did you include all the information you're going to require in your information request line?

When you're happy with everything, press **Save,** and your gig will go live.

Pretty simple, right?

Here are a few things you should keep in mind as you begin your career on Fiverr:

- Sellers can list a maximum of twenty gigs at one time. Choose the gigs you offer carefully. Make sure they are gigs you can complete the quickest and that will sell the best.

- When you are first starting out, you're only allowed to offer two gig extras, but many sellers have found a clever way around this. They suggest buyers should purchase an additional gig if they want something extra. For example, if your gig is to write a 200-word SEO article for $5.00, you could mention that buyers "should purchase an extra gig for every additional 200 words." It gives you the same benefit as being able to offer a gig extra.

- Be careful about the types of gigs you offer. Reviews and testimonials are big business on Fiverr, but offering to write a bogus book or product reviews for Amazon items is against Amazon's terms of service. What you will discover is many of these reviewers have a very short lifespan on Fiverr because they quickly get shut down.

- Always offer great value for the money you are charging. It will come back to you with good reviews and more business over the long haul.

- Spend at least a half-hour every week checking through the gigs offered on Fiverr. Watch for new trends and services you may not currently be offering. It will help you to grow your business and keep your offerings fresh and relevant.

Fiverr Selling 101

Fiverr continues to reinvent itself as the freelance marketplace evolves. Gigs are no longer required to start at $5.00, but most buyers offer a $5.00 gig as a gateway to more expensive offerings.

We've already talked about gig extras. Depending upon your seller level, they give you an amazing opportunity to boost your income while customizing your gigs to meet buyer wants and needs.

Package attributes are a relatively new feature that can boost your sales.

If you've spent any time on Fiverr, you probably know what I'm talking about—even if you don't recognize the name.

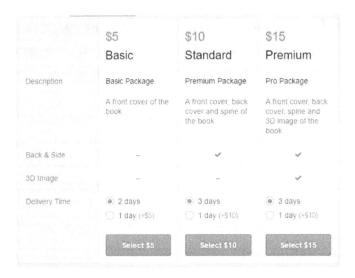

	$5	$10	$15
	Basic	Standard	Premium
Description	Basic Package	Premium Package	Pro Package
	A front cover of the book	A front cover, back cover and spine of the book	A front cover, back cover, spine and 3D image of the book
Back & Side	–	✓	✓
3D Image	–	–	✓
Delivery Time	◉ 2 days ◯ 1 day (+$5)	◉ 3 days ◯ 1 day (+$10)	◉ 3 days ◯ 1 day (+$10)
	Select $5	Select $10	Select $15

What I like about package attributes is they make it easy for buyers to compare your offerings. You can offer a basic product for $5.00, a step-up for $25.00, and a bigger step-up for $50.00. Most sellers are going to pick the middle option. They don't want to go too cheap, but they don't want to blow their whole wad either.

Package attributes make it easier to convert lookers into buyers because you're offering them more choices. I don't have any specific proof, but my guess is package attributes convert better than gig extras.

Experiment with your listings and discover what works best for you.

Custom Offers are where the real money is on Fiverr. Forbes Magazine did a story about four sellers who make $15,000 a month or more by using custom offers. One of the ladies profiled in the article runs an executive resume writing service. She went from making $5.00 per gig to making over $300,000 last year. A lot of her business comes from creating custom resume packages and selling them for $500 to $800 each—all by sending custom offers.

Think you can't do it? Think again.

Suppose you are a graphic designer who sells custom book covers on Fiverr. Create your listing just as you normally would. Add package attributes and gig extras to up-sell regular buyers. The only thing I want you to do differently is to add an additional line at the top and bottom of your item description page. It can be as simple as, "Are you looking for an eye-shattering design? Contact me for a *Custom Offer*."

That throws it back into the buyer's court. Some of them are going to be curious and contact you. When they do, ask a few well-placed discovery questions and fire off an offer to let them know what you can do for them.

Fiverr Anywhere works hand in hand with *Custom Offers* to help you make larger dollar sales.

Fiverr Anywhere started out as a Google Chrome extension. Since then, it has moved to the Fiverr site. To access *Fiverr Anywhere,* go to the Promote Your Business section under the My Sales Tab. Click on the Generate *Custom Offer* tab, then create your custom offer. After you've done that, you can retrieve your link. That will let you add your offer to your website, blog, email, or social media sites.

When someone contacts you, it works just like a regular *Custom Offer*. Potential buyers can accept your offer or request a modification.

Use *Fiver Anywhere* and *Custom Offer* to grow your business and reach new buyers off the Fiverr website.